MY LIFE EXPERIENCES
ON THE ROAD TO BECOMING AND BEING A MINISTER IN
THE CHURCH OF JESUS CHRIST

by

ANTHONY J. MICALE
Ordained Minister

the Peppertree Press
Sarasota, Florida

The Church of Jesus Christ is not affiliated with the LDS, Latter Day Saints, Church or any other organization; with headquarters in Monogahala, PA 15063

Copyright © Anthony J. Micale, 2013

All rights reserved. Published by the Peppertree Press, LLC. the Peppertree Press and associated logos are trademarks of the Peppertree Press, LLC.

No part of this publication may be reproduced, stored in a retrieval system, transmitted in any form or by any means, electronic, mechanical, photocopying, recording, or otherwise, without prior written permission of the publisher and author/illustrator. Graphic design by Rebecca Barbier.

For information regarding permission,
call 941-922-2662 or contact us at our website:
www.peppertreepublishing.com or write to:
the Peppertree Press, LLC.
Attention: Publisher
1269 First Street, Suite 7
Sarasota, Florida 34236

ISBN: 978-1-61493-135-5

Library of Congress Number: 2012921971

Printed in the U.S.A.

Printed January 2013

As you read these pages...

THIS WRITING IS NOT INTENDED TO BOAST ABOUT my life, but to praise my Maker for his goodness and great mercy to me.

When we start out in life, none of us knows what is in store for us. The choices we make early in life determine who we are and what we will become. Looking back I would have made a lot of other choices and done some things differently. Each of us needs to think clearly about each step we take in life. I wish I had thought more clearly about my personal life—you will know what I mean as you read on. The Gospel of Jesus Christ and my family pulled me through. These joys were the most precious parts of my life. For reasons I cannot explain, the Lord has watched over me and has seen me through the difficult times, which were many.

May our Gracious Heavenly Father bless you and draw you close to Him and His Son, Jesus—and to your own family—as you read my story.

*"But as for me, I will always have hope;
I will praise you more and more.
My mouth will tell of your righteousness,
of your salvation all day long,
though I know not its measure.
I will come and proclaim your mighty acts,
O Sovereign Lord;
I will proclaim your righteousness,
Yours alone. Since my youth,
O God you have taught me,
and to this day I declare your marvelous deeds.
Even when I am old and gray
do not forsake me, O God,
'Til I declare your power to the next generation, your
might to all who are to come.*

*Your righteousness reaches to the skies,
O God, you who have done great things.
Who, O God, is like you?
Though you have made me see troubles,
many and bitter, you will restore my life again;
from the depths of the earth
you will again bring it up.
You will increase my honor and comfort me
once again."*

Psalm 71, vs. 14-21 (NIV)

FROM MY DAUGHTER, LINDA, AND HER HUSBAND, JEFF,
WHILE READING SCRIPTURES ON TOP OF
INDEPENDENCE PASS, COLORADO
AUGUST 2012

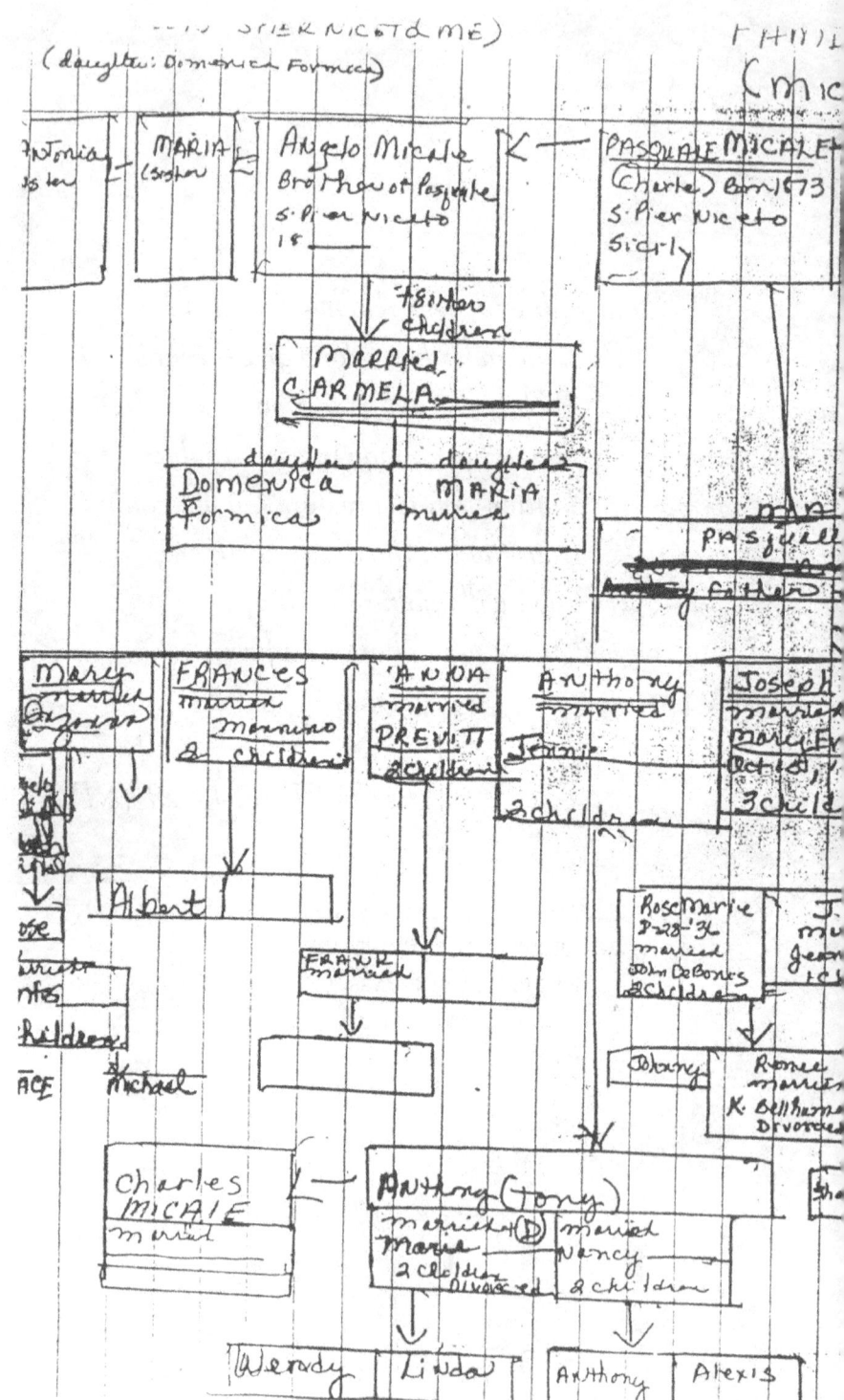

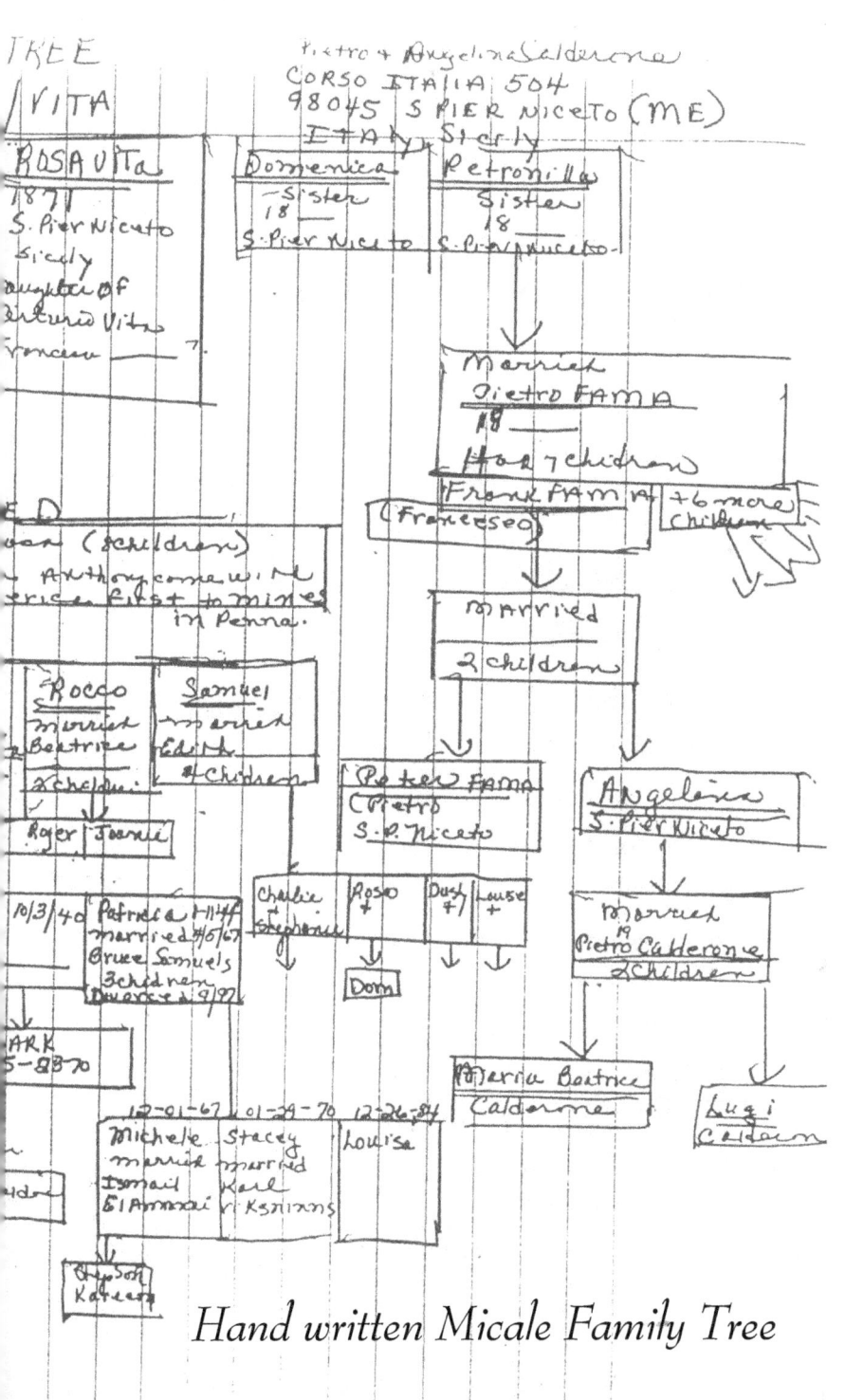

Hand written Micale Family Tree

Table of Contents

The Beginning of My Road	1
"I Know the Plans I Have For You," Says the Lord	13
"God Works Out All Things for Good" – My Family	19
The Lord Established the Work of My Hands	37
Just Another Bend in the Road	45
Sing Glory – The Lord has Done Wonderful Things	49
Come Sit with Us	50
Unless the Lord Builds the House…	52
Supporting the Church in Tampa, Florida	57
I Will Never Leave You or Forsake You	59
A Nigerian Home in Memory of My Mother and Father	61
The Joy of Being Used to Fill a Need	63
The Lord is My Strength An Amazing Story of God's Rescue	68
Building a Branch in South Jersey The Lord's Timing	71
The Beginning of Our Family's Work in Italy	73

*Anthony Micale, Sr. Birth Place
— San Pier Niceto, Italy (Sicily)*

Wendy Ann Goes Home	75
A Blessing Even in a Time of Sorrow	79
The Lord Answers Prayers in Italy	81
The Enemy Prowls Around Like a Roaring Lion	84
More of God's Blessings in Italy	86
It Will Not Harm Them	88
Come and See — The Lord's Work in Florida	91
In Honor of Coleen, Lydia's Mother	95
Jesus Never Fails - On Becoming a Minister in the Church of Jesus Christ	97
His Love and Mercy Overflows	107
A Wonder, A Marvel	115

On August 28, 2011, I was ordained into the ministry as an Elder in the Church of Jesus Christ. This was the beginning of my fiftieth year in the Gospel of Jesus Christ, since I was baptized on August 4, 1962. One might ask the question, "What took so long"? You might say that timing is everything, especially the Lord's timing. The road to my ordination was filled with successes, trials, and failures, just as many of us experience in life. But as the old hymn says, "Jesus never fails."

Over the years, I have been encouraged by friends, Brothers and Sisters in the Church, and my family to write down my experiences in life and in the Church. This writing is an attempt to highlight some of the most eventful moments on this road with Jesus Christ. As my family and friends have expressed to me many times, my life has not been dull. It has been painful at times, then joyful, but <u>never</u> dull.

The Beginning of My Road

EVERY ROAD HAS A BEGINNING, SO ALLOW ME TO start mine with my family coming to America. My grandparents on both sides of the family lived in rural Italy. My father, Anthony Micale, was born in San Pier Niceto, a small town on the side of Mt. Etna in Sicily, on February 14, 1898. Life was hard and they were poor, so like many at the turn of the 20th century, both sides of my family emigrated from Europe to the United States. My father was 14 years old when he and his father arrived at Ellis Island in New York in 1912. My daughter, Linda, tells me that when she asked her Grandpa why they left Italy, he answered, "You can't eat scenery!" My mother, Giovanna (Jennie) Sgro, was born here in the States after their family arrived in America.

I don't know much about that time, because my family really wanted to be American and my father didn't marry my mother until he was 36 years old. What I do know is that somewhere, we still have a worn copy of the U.S. history book from 1898

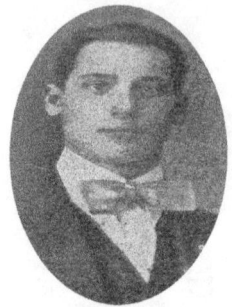

Anthony Micale, Sr

that my father used to study for his citizenship and I know he was proud of his new country. We have an old family photograph showing my grandparents and all eight of their children once they arrived in America. I know that my father and grandfather worked in the coal mines of Pennsylvania. Some years later, when my father was still a young man, he studied voice and became an opera singer. He came from a very talented and musical family. My father had a beautiful voice and sang in Carnegie Hall in New York in the 1920s.

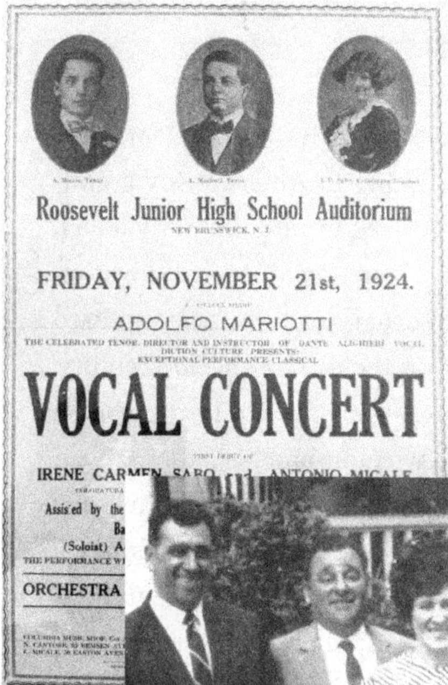

Roosevelt Junior High School Auditorium

NEW BRUNSWICK, N. J.

FRIDAY, NOVEMBER 21st, 1924.

ADOLFO MARIOTTI

THE CELEBRATED TENOR, DIRECTOR AND INSTRUCTOR OF DANTE ALIGHIERI VOCAL DICTION CULTURE PRESENTS: EXCEPTIONAL PERFORMANCE CLASSICAL

VOCAL CONCERT

IRENE CARMEN SARO and ANTONIO MICALE

Assisted by the

(Soloist) A

ORCHESTRA

We still have a program from one of my father's performances in New Jersey. Sadly, my father became ill with stomach problems that affected his breathing, so he had to give up singing in performances, but he never lost his love of music.

My father, Anthony, became acquainted with the

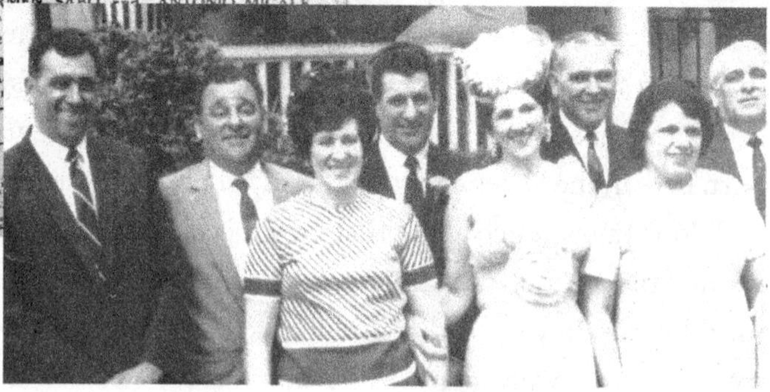

The Sgro Family on mother's side

Church of Jesus Christ when his sister, Mary Micale, married Rocco Ensana. Uncle Rocco was a Church member in New Jersey who loved telling people about Jesus. My mother's family was already part of the Church. When Uncle Rocco shared the Gospel with my father, he started attending too. It was in the Church that my father and mother met and got to know one another. My mother was one of the kindest and most loving women you could ever find.

My mother's sister, Mary Sgro, now in her mid-90s, recently told me a story of my parents' courtship. In those days "rules"

The Micale Family

*Tony and Ester Sgro
Grandfather & Grandmother*

*Uncle Angelo and
my father, Anthony (twins)*

My mother, Jennie (center) and Aunt Mary (on the right)

Sgro & Ensana, Micale Family

of society required that a couple had a chaperone to go anywhere. Mary Sgro was often that chaperone for my father and mother, but for a quarter, my father asked Aunt Mary if she would leave them alone for a while! They were always "alone" in a public place, of course, but it is still a sweet memory of my father's love for my mother. That love continued through the years. My daughter, Linda, recalls how her Grandpa (my father) would always say about her Grammie, "She's the best girl in town"—and she surely was.

My parents, Anthony and Jennie, were married in 1934 in the Church. My father was already in his 30s at the time, but my mother was much younger. On October 6, 1935, they had a son named Charles, my older brother. I was born in New Brunswick, New Jersey on November 27, 1937. My brother Charles and I were fortunate enough to have a good head start

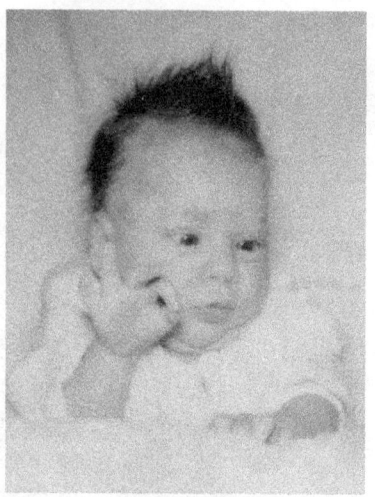

Picture of me at a few months old

My brother Charles and Me (on right)

with God-fearing parents, who brought us up in the right way.

In the early years of our family, my father was a shoe repair man and later learned the sewing machine repair business. We lived in Newark, New Jersey, where my father worked until I was 12 years old. We traveled to the Bronx, New York mission of the Church on Sundays by train. In 1949, we moved to Edison, New Jersey, to be near the rest of our relatives and the Church. My father commuted back to the city of Newark each day about 20 miles by train until he retired. He was a skilled sewing machine mechanic in the garment industry, where he worked long hours. I enjoyed the times he would take me with him to work and we could spend time together. Our vacations were mostly going to Church functions and visiting family and friends in the Church. Church was our life, which helped to root me in the Gospel.

Micale Family

I recall my father and mother telling stories about how hard it was in those early years just to put food on the table. My parents lived through the Depression in 1929 and worked very hard to provide a home for us. My father was hard-working and

Me at 10 years old on my bicycle built from junk

My mother, Jennie and father, Anthony at our home in Edison, NJ

disciplined. He would give you the shirt off his back. He loved us, but you knew he was the head of the household. Respect was everything to him. You never answered him back. In those days, family was everything and children were "seen, but not heard."

Fashion is a word we did not understand or know when I was young. I had one suit and two pairs of shoes, one for Sunday and one for school. Those shoes were repaired until they no longer fit on my feet. I remember my first bicycle was made from parts of two other bikes that were junk. I learned the word, "work," early in life. We did not have much in material things, but they gave us what a family needs most, a God-fearing and loving home.

From the age of 12 to 17 years old, I held part-time jobs in a dairy farm, delivering newspapers before I went to school and working for my uncle in his music store. Everyone pitched in. Money was tight, so if you wanted something, you earned the money to get it. Nothing was wasted in our house. We planted a garden each year and the food we grew was canned for the winter. Home-grown tomato sauce was my favorite.

My Uncle Sam Micale, my first real job as a music store salesman

*Brother Charles, Mother and Me
Newark, NJ 1948*

Backyard of Aunt Anna Micale's house in the 1930's

My brother Charles, my Father and Me, 1948

My father made a wise investment in a three-story apartment building in Newark, New Jersey, when we lived there. It had stores on the first floor and we lived on the second floor, so the rental income paid for the building. The sale of this property helped provide the money to build a new home in Edison, New Jersey, and retirement money for my parents. In the years to come, this very same money would be used to help us start out in the McDonald's business.

I loved my parents with all my heart. Their experiences are the foundation for my own; the threads of their lives are woven throughout mine as my story continues. My father died at 77 years old in 1975 of a heart attack and my mother passed away at 69 years old of a cancerous brain tumor in 1980. They both died too young, on the same day, February 14th, and were buried on the 18th, which was my father's birthday. I thank God for the legacy of my mother and father—loving God and working hard for what is really important.

Daughters Wendy Ann and Linda

Me and Marie

"I know the plans I have for you," says the Lord

I WAS MARRIED RIGHT OUT OF HIGH SCHOOL ON February 16, 1957 at the age of nineteen. By the time I was 21 years old, we had two wonderful daughters, Linda and Wendy Ann. I had completed a four-year apprentice program to become a union sheet metal worker, bought my first new house, completed a four-year tour in the National Guard, and started my part-time career with McDonald's.

This was the normal course of events in the 1950s after graduating high school. You would find a job and get married, if you did not go to college. At that time college was for becoming doctors, lawyers, or engineers. The trades or manufacturing were where most people went to work. A higher education was not what I wanted for my life. My high school teacher told me that if I did not get a job selling, it would be a big mistake. Indirectly, I have been doing that, by selling my ability to work hard, deliver results, do my best to get along with others, and have a positive attitude in whatever I do.

After working at a low-paying job, I looked for opportunities and was fortunate to learn the sheet metal worker trade. I attended four years of night school to become a union journeyman, which paid very well. In 1959 I was transferred from New Jersey to Huntington Station, Long Island, New York, where the company I was working for had a lot of work. We purchased our first house there for $13,300.00; it was a small Cape Cod-style house with four rooms, an attic and a basement. Our daughters, Linda and Wendy Ann, were a joy in our lives. Linda was the one who always aimed to please and did. Wendy Ann kept us on our toes and made us laugh and cry a lot.

I looked for a part-time job so we could build a dormer for the attic, which would cost $500. I saw a "Now Hiring" sign for a new McDonald's that was being built in town. That McDonald's sign is still etched in my mind. I started working there at night after my job as a union sheet metal worker during the day. I continued to work both jobs for the next few years. I thought I knew the plans I had for our lives together, but God had another plan in mind.

The year 1962 was one of the most remarkable on the road of my life. In that year, I convinced my father to invest all of his retirement money in purchasing a new McDonald's. While we were in the process of discussing this, my father and mother visited us and told me about a new mission in Lake Ronkonkoma, Long Island, New York. They asked me if I would visit this new mission with them and I agreed. I was raised in the Church, but I was not a member. I had not yet given my life to Jesus Christ. Brother Salvatore Valenti, an Elder of the Church, had built a small church in his backyard. It was in the middle of his garden and it was the most humble place I had ever seen. It was about 10-feet by 10-feet with a few chairs and a potbelly stove in the corner. His meetings were generally attended by his wife, Sister Anna, who was blind, and maybe one or two others at most. It was one of the most Spirit-filled meetings I had ever attended. The Lord truly was in this building. My parents returned to New Jersey that weekend, but I continued to visit this small mission in the garden. The sincerity and faithfulness of those few members in that humble place touched my heart. I felt the Spirit of God so strongly calling me into the Gospel that I could not hold myself back. I stood up crying out that I wanted to be baptized in the Church of Jesus Christ. I praise God that salvation was given to me on that day, August 4, 1962. I was 24 years old.

Meanwhile, working two jobs began to take a toll on my health. Three months after my baptism, I learned that I had a deadly disease called tuberculosis (TB). The Lord knew what was ahead for me. I had been working two jobs to save money for home improvements and did not take care of myself for over three and a half years. There was no cure for TB in those days. When I went to the doctor, he told me it was just a bad cold and gave me medicine. He then took a few tests and sent me home to rest. I returned to the doctor, because I wasn't getting well; he told me that I had a very bad sore throat and took some samples of my throat fluid and again sent me home to recover. A few days later, I answered a knock at the door and was met by two social workers with masks on their faces. They told me I had a very bad case of tuberculosis (TB). Without any warning, the social workers took me to a Sanatorium in Farmingdale, Long Island, New York. This was quite a shock. I was told I could infect New York City with one breath. After an x-ray was taken, they found holes in my lungs the size of quarters and more tests showed that my body was wracked with the disease. I had lost a lot of weight and the outlook was grim.

I was bleeding from my mouth; the disease was throughout my lungs. Life for me was finished, or so I thought. I was not given much hope, and even if I managed to live, it was doubtful that I would ever have sufficient strength for a meaningful life. Despite all of this, the Lord had a different plan for me. Once the Church and my parents found out about my illness, the full benefit of the Church of Jesus Christ went into action.

Special prayer meetings were held and I can still hear my father singing the hymn, "He Lives", in one of the services in the Edison branch of the Church. Some of these meetings were recorded on reel-to-reel tape and sent to me to encourage me. Three Elders came to the Sanatorium to visit and anoint me with oil by laying on of hands as we are told in the Bible to do. Their names were Brother Dominick Rose, Brother Salvatore Valenti, and Brother James Link. They encouraged me and told me to have faith in God. Jesus Christ is truly a rock in a time of storm.

About a week later, I was tested by the hospital and they found the disease gone completely and the holes in my lungs healed with no scars. God is the same yesterday, today and forever. The Lord had performed a miracle and spared my life. The doctors were in disbelief. They kept me in the Sanatorium for six months because it was the law for observation. Those six months in the Sanatorium were counted by me as a blessing. During those months, the Lord grounded me in the Gospel in a way that I would never forget Him. I think back now and realize that this foundation from my time in the Sanatorium gave me the strength to go through the trials of life I was going to face. There I studied the Scriptures and read them from beginning to end. I felt the Spirit of God so strong during this time in my life that it is hard to explain. I had dreams and experiences that I will never forget. Although my very existence was threatened, this was a special time in my life. I felt so close to the Lord, and it was beautiful. I wonder what would have happened if I had not answered the call to be baptized three months earlier. What would I have done? Who would I have turned to? It is obvious to me now that the Lord spared my life, because HE had work for me to do for Him in my life.

Linda and Wendy Ann

Wendy Ann, Me and Linda

"God Works Out All Things for Good"

My Family

BEFORE I CONTINUE TO DESCRIBE MY WORK AT McDonald's and for the Lord, I would like to share more about my beloved children and my family life.

As I mentioned earlier, in the early years of our marriage, my first wife and I had two daughters, Linda and Wendy Ann. I can't say I was prepared at that young age for the most important job in my life—raising children—but by the grace of God, somehow we got through it.

My daughters were both very close to me and we attended Church together whenever we could, since we lived far away from the closest branch. I remember the fun times we had together on some of our vacations. The first was a trip to Niagara Falls, New York in 1965. The next trip was a three-week trip by car to tour the United States in the summer of 1967. I purchased our first air-conditioned car for that trip because we were all scared about crossing the legendary Mohave Desert on our way to southern California! It was a trip filled with memories of our family's first experience of the U.S. coast-to-coast. Some years later, our last big family trip was a three-week tour of Europe. Linda wrote a journal about that trip and we have it on film.

Sadly, my marriage to Linda and Wendy Ann's mother ended in 1978 after 21 years. Strong differences in religion and personalities played a big part in our breakup. I deeply regret my part in the pain of this time. Looking back, I wish my wife and I had spent more time getting to know each other before we got married, especially since we were very young. I didn't know at the time we married, how important my faith would become. Since then I have learned that anyone considering marriage should be very sure that they can accept or share the religious beliefs of their future husband or wife.

When my first marriage broke up, I made some bad choices and mistakes as I struggled with finding my place in life. Consequently, the next several years after this divorce were very difficult for all of us. This is one of those times on the road of my life that I wish I had thought more clearly. It took several years before I was able to get my life back on track again.

The hardest thing for me besides the effect on the children was the lost of my membership in the Church of Jesus Christ. At that time, divorce was unheard of in the Church. Nevertheless, I continued to attend the Church meetings faithfully, but it wasn't easy. I felt this problem was mine and my service to the Lord must continue.

In 1980, I married again and we had two more equally wonderful children, Anthony III and Alexis. I remember how excited I was when Anthony was born. I yelled from one end of the

MY LIFE EXPERIENCES ON THE ROAD...

Pike's Peak at 23 years old

Alexis, Anthony III and I

Son, Anthony Micale III

Anthony and Alexis Micale

hospital to the other. Every father wants a son and I was no different. While Anthony was growing up, he would walk around with a suit, tie and briefcase—always a business man! He also has a great mind for figuring out how things work and a natural curiosity. Alexis was like Wendy Ann, beautiful and extraverted, and she kept me on my toes. There never was a dull moment with Alexis. Growing up, she had her own mind and a huge heart.

I have wonderful memories of the times I had with Anthony and Alexis as children. We traveled extensively all over the world on ship cruises and in Europe. During the summers, we spent a lot of time at the New Jersey shore, first in Margate and then in Longport, New Jersey. We built a beautiful home on the water in Longport and really enjoyed the summers boating and going to the beach. After the children were out on their own, the house in Longport, New Jersey, was too big and we eventually sold it.

During my second marriage, Church leadership opened the door for me to be reinstated as a member. By that time, it had been 16 years since my divorce, but I continued to get up, choose Christ, and attend Church, even though

Anthony and Alexis

Alexis and Wendy Ann

Longport, New Jersey, Summer Home

I couldn't participate in many of the Church's ordinances. Continuing to attend the Church was one of the best decisions I have ever made in my life. It wasn't my own strength or merit, I can tell you that. I can see now how this was a picture of God's grace: even though I made terrible mistakes in life, He loved me still and helped me back up when I turned to Him.

Then in 1999, life changed dramatically. Once again, I am sorry to say that my marriage to Anthony and Alexis' mother ended after 20 years, even after doing all I could to save it. I realized too late that good communication is critical in a marriage and that it was lacking in ours. There are times in your life when things are out of your control and this was one of those times. I took this breakup very hard and it took me a long time to get over it. This divorce was not my choice and I was very depressed. Day after day, I was on my knees praying and asking the Lord to help me. My children were concerned for my health. I felt my life was over, but the Lord had other plans for me that was so much more than I could have asked or imagined.

I thank God that when I was at my lowest point, I met my wife, Lydia, unexpectedly through mutual friends in Florida. Lydia was a single mom, focused on raising her beautiful eight-year-old daughter, Chiara. She hadn't dated much since her own divorce some years earlier and initially, she didn't even want to join our mutual friends for dinner the evening that she and I met! Yet Lydia impressed me right away and she was just what the doctor ordered at this time in my life. She and I could talk about everything and for hours; that type of open, honest communication was something completely new to me. Later during

Chiara and Lydia

Lydia and Me

our courtship, I began to see that Lydia was accepting of our Church, learned that she spoke Italian, and had even lived in Italy for a time! At 61 years of age, I found myself starting a new life again and the Lord had seen me through once more.

Yet I still did not know what a blessing Lydia would be to me in the Church and as a wife. We were married in 2001 in Sarasota, Florida, surrounded by our children. When we married, it was Lydia who had a deep recognition that we were bringing three families together. She made a beautiful home that is welcoming and loving to all of our children and to friends and family that often visit. After a few years, in 2005, the Lord called Lydia into the Gospel while we were attending the Church in Levittown, PA. I was ecstatic to fully share this wonderful Gospel road with my wife. Five years later in 2010, Lydia was ordained a Deaconess in the Church in Florida at special service at the Cape Coral mission. In addition, her Italian language skills became a great benefit to us in missionary work in Italy that has become one of the passions of our life that I'll write more about later in my story. All along, the Lord had a plan for us and provided for my need. Lydia is indeed a great gift and a joy in my life.

I am also thankful for my stepdaughter, Chiara, Lydia's daughter, who keeps reminding me of what it is like to be young. As I mentioned, Chiara was eight years old when we met and she was an only child. A year or so later on the night in 2000 when Lydia and I were engaged, my children 'proposed' to Chiara to ask her if she wanted to be part of our family. We are so glad that she too said, 'Yes.' In the years that followed with little Chiara in our home, I got a lot of training in patience, which I have needed as a much older person! Now

Lydia and My Wedding

Chiara and Me

it is 2012 and Chiara has turned 21. She is attending Emerson College in Boston to become a broadcast journalist. Lydia and I are both very proud of her accomplishments.

If anyone would have told me years ago I would be going through two divorces and be married three times, I would have told them that they must be crazy. I do not recommend that hard road to anyone, as it brings times that are extremely difficult to live through. I regret the harm these trials in my life have had on my children. Thank God, for the most part, they have gotten through it and we now live in peace and love together, which is a blessing from God.

Chiara, step-daughter

Anthony and Alexis have both received an excellent education, which is so important in today's world. Anthony graduated from Babson College in Boston, one of the best business schools in the country. Alexis graduated from American University in Washington, DC with a Masters Degree in Business, with a minor in Communications. Alexis is still strong and accomplished and has a wonderful, joyful warmth and love of life. More important than this, Anthony and Alexis are both happily married and our extended family is growing. Alexis married our son-in-law, Steven D'Achille, in October 2009. Anthony married our daughter-in-law, Jennifer, in February 2011 and we are anxiously awaiting the birth of our first grandchild!

Jeff, Tyler and Linda

Linda's Wedding Party

Jeff, Linda and Tyler

Linda and I still have a wonderful loving relationship. I remember the day she was baptized in 1972 in the Church at a campout in New Hope, New Jersey. Linda graduated from the University of Arizona with a Masters Degree in Renewable Natural Resources. She is one of the best in the business. At one point in her career, Linda started and ran her own environmental consulting business for four years. Linda had some difficult years away from the Lord in her 20s and 30s, but over time and by God's grace, she returned to her faith and now serves Him. She is happily married now to Jeff and has a 22-year old stepson named Tyler, who is a joy to be around. They all love the Lord as a family.

I am sad to say that Wendy Ann passed away at a young age of a heart problem in 2006—she is greatly missed. Wendy Ann always loved the Lord and had just completed law school. She would have been a great lawyer. No one could win a debate with

Anthony III and Jennifer Micale Wedding

Tony, Anthony, Jennifer and Nancy

her! Although she and I didn't always see eye to eye, she was a very special daughter to me. I will write more on this later on.

I can't leave the subject of our family without thanking all the special friends and Brothers and Sisters in the Church who walked with me on this road. Among these dearly beloved friends, I want to thank Brother Apostle Paul Benyola and Sister Dottie Benyola. Through all those years and hard times, they were by my side, encouraging and coaching me. They have been best friends to our family and we are very thankful for their support and love.

The Bible says, "And we know that all things work together for good to those who love God, to those who are the called according to His purpose." (Romans 8:28) God used all the joys and sorrows of these years for ultimate good in our lives. One of the things I am happiest about is that the Lord has used me and my family's testimony to bring some of our other family

Paul and Dottie Benyola

Steven and Alexis

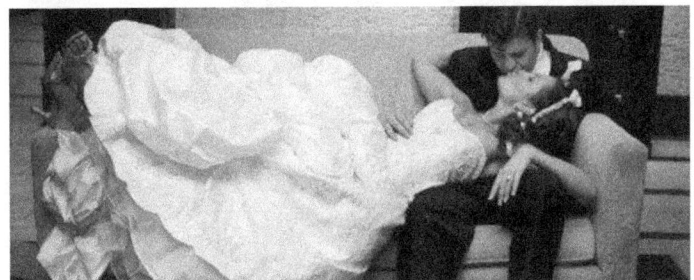

Alexis and Steven

*My Daughter and Son-in-Law,
Alexis and Steven D'Achille*

*Alexis, Anthony, Tony and Chiara,
Family vacation in Paris, France, 2001*

*Alexis and Steven
D'Achille*

*Anthony and Jennifer
Micale III*

members and acquaintances to whom we have talked into the Gospel of Jesus Christ. I think how the Lord said that we hide a multitude of sins when we bring someone into the Gospel and a soul is saved. "Brethren, if anyone among you wanders from the truth, and someone turns him back, let him know that he who turns a sinner from the error of his way will save a soul from death and cover a multitude of sins." (James 5:19-20) "And above all things have fervent love for one another, for love will cover a multitude of sins." (1 Peter 4:8) I can truly say love is greatly at work in our family, healing the hurts, bringing new joys, and building future memories.

The Micale Family 2005

McDonald's Opening in 1963

The Lord Established the Work of My Hands

LIKE SO MUCH IN MY LIFE, THE STORY OF MY CAreer with McDonald's begins with family. If I may, I'd like to pick up where I left off back in late 1950s to early 1960s. Before I became ill with TB, I had convinced my father to invest all the retirement money he received from selling that apartment house in Newark, New Jersey, to start a McDonald's franchise. My thought was to bring our entire family together in business. I had learned this business during my four years working in a McDonald's part-time on Long Island, New York. When I started this job in 1959 for an hourly wage of $1.00, Ray Kroc, the founder of McDonald's, was just starting to build the brand. That McDonald's in Long Island had lines out the door and I saw the tremendous opportunity for entering this new company. Dad must have seen that too, but he took quite a risk for his sons—he was 65 years old at that time.

In 1962, my brother Charles, who lived in Texas at the time, and I went to Chicago to see Ray at his office. It was the size of my living room now. The original founders of the business were there: Ray Kroc, Fred Turner, June Martino and Harry Sonneborn. I said, "Ray, I have worked for almost four years in the business and we would like a franchise." He said to me, "Do you have any money? I said, "Yes." Ray responded, "Then you have a franchise!" That seemed to settle it!

As a result of that meeting, we bought a franchise in Binghamton, New York. In the meantime, I fell ill with TB. Our McDonald's was under construction and my father and brother started the business. At that time, I thought I would never join them. As you now have read, the Lord healed me of the disease and I was able to return to my life and our new business. Since then, I have never looked back. Thank God, I did choose this path, but it wasn't an easy road.

We opened the first store in April of 1963. Those first few years in Binghamton were a big disappointment. Upstate New York was not Long Island. This was a rural area; we were unknown and people there were not used to eating hamburgers! Opening day we did $168.00 in sales. We worked eighteen-hour days in the early years to get things going. We struggled to pay the bills and could not make the rent payments to McDonald's for a long time. We all worked hard and in the next seven years, we opened six more stores in the area as the concept of McDonald's started to catch on.

Unfortunately, this took us all away from the nearest branch of the Church of Jesus Christ. My father, mother, and my brother, Charles, and his family were there as well. For a while, Brother Joe Perri and his family came to try and start a new work for the Church in Upstate New York, but it was not to be. In addition, we struggled for many years with the Church law, in force at the time, regarding no business on Sunday.

The franchise required that we stay open seven days a week. Thankfully, the Church has since removed that law, but it is another example of one of the difficulties of our early years in business and trying to stay true to the Church. We tried our best to serve God and visited the branches in New Jersey when we could.

We had also started building new McDonald's stores in the late 60s at the request of McDonald's Corporation in Philadelphia, Pennsylvania. Our agreement with the Corporation was they would allow us to build 25 stores over a five-year period and then sell those stores back to them. The McDonald's system started to grow rapidly and owner-operators, like us, helped speed up that growth. We sold the New York stores in 1970 to fund and concentrate on building stores in the Philadelphia market. The good news with this sale was we sold the stores mostly for McDonald's stock, which tripled in value over the next few years after the New York stores were sold. My brother, Charles, and I built sixteen stores in eighteen months in Philadelphia. This is still a record in McDonald's today for an owner/operator.

In 1971, our families moved to the Philadelphia area to manage the business in Philadelphia. Two years later, we decided to sell most of the stores in Philadelphia back to the McDonald's Corporation, which was always the plan. What wasn't part of that plan was that my brother, Charles, left the McDonald's system. By this time, my father had also sold his part in the business to us. After my brother left to pursue another business, I continued on my own to build and purchase over twenty more McDonald's stores over the next 40 years.

During those early years, our combined families built and

Cherry Hill, New Jersey Home

operated over 23 McDonald's stores and were responsible for starting two new regions for McDonald's Corporation in upstate New York and Philadelphia, Pennsylvania. McDonald's was green and growing in those days. Now in 2012, I still work the business at age 74 and have 52 years in the McDonald's system. I have been involved in owning and operating over 42 McDonald's stores so far in my career, which gives me a real sense of pride and accomplishment. I still serve as Chair of the Finance Committee and Treasurer of the Co-Op, the organization for Philadelphia region owners and operators. There is so much to tell about how the Lord blessed us through McDonald's and there are so many milestones I could write about. Here are just a few examples...

In 1974, the Lord gave us a beautiful home in New Jersey that had been built by Muhammad Ali, who was the world heavy-weight champion at that time. There was a lot of excitement about this house then, as there still is today. Many newspaper and magazine stories have been written about the house and our family. It has been eventful living there on Winding

MY LIFE EXPERIENCES ON THE ROAD...

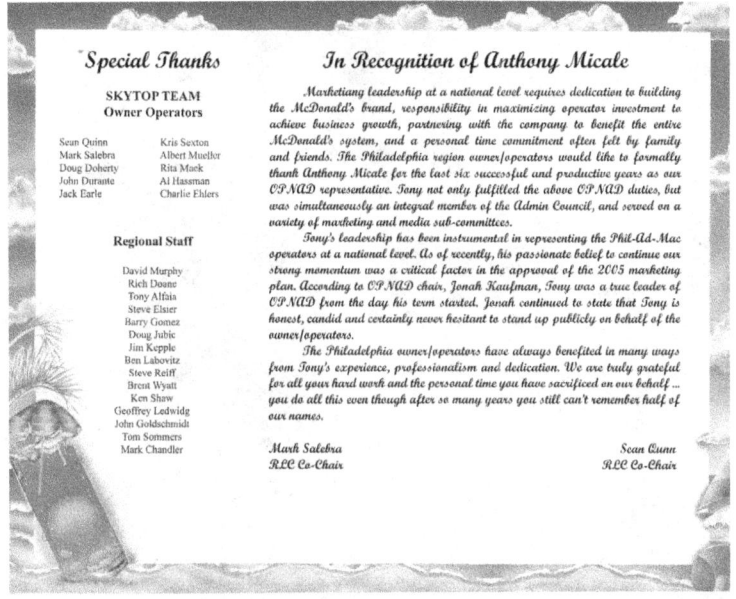

Drive raising three different families. I could write a book just on the events that occurred in this house. One day soon, we hope to sell it and live more simply, but that doesn't take away the significance this home has had for everyone in our family.

I have held many positions and served as chairman of various committees in McDonald's that have had a major impact on the Corporation. There are two examples that I am especially proud of. As Co-Op President of the Operators Association, we approved the *first* Ronald McDonald House for children in Philadelphia in 1975. Today there are hundreds of Ronald McDonald Houses all over the world! Thousands of children and families have benefited from these wonderful houses for sick children. When I was a member of McDonald's National Advertising Administrative Council, we pushed through the very popular dollar menu in the McDonald system. The dollar

41

50 Years of Service Celebration in Atlantic City, New Jersey, 2010

menu was the spearhead for the new "Plan to Win" that put McDonald's back on a strong sales growth track.

In 2010, I will never forget and I am so thankful for the huge celebration that McDonald's Corporation hosted to recognize me for 50 years of service. This celebration was during a convention being held Atlantic City, New Jersey, for owner-operators, with over 550 people in attendance! I am happy to say most of my family and friends attended. Linda could not attend but wrote me a beautiful letter congratulating me and noting the things she remembered about being a "McDonald's kid" while she was growing up.

I lived and watched the McDonald's system grow from nothing to what it is today, a 35-billion-dollar business all over the world. No one would have believed it in the late 1950s. McDonald's is bigger than the next five competitors combined. There were many ups and downs in the business and we worked very hard for many years. I am grateful to God for the vision he gave me to see this great opportunity and for the risk my father took. The Lord has certainly established the work of my hands, as the Bible says in Psalm 90. But now I am hopeful that in the near future I can devote more of my time to building the Kingdom of God here on earth.

REPRINTED FROM "POWERBOAT MAGAZINE" MAY, 1982, PAGE 24.

With all due respect to offshore giants Wellcraft, Thunderbird, Cigarette, Magnum, Chris-Craft and Fountain Powerboats, as far as we're concerned, the very best offshore sportboat on the water today is the Excalibur Hawk. We were so overwhelmed with this sensational new 40-footer that we'd even go so far as to say that Excalibur has produced the finest offshore machine ever.

Competing against the very finest of the high-dollar set, Excalibur's new 40-foot Hawk buried the competition in our Offshore Boat of the Year challenge. Immediately after we concluded this year's third annual big-boat evaluations in Sarasota, Fla., we polled the staff on its choice for the number one slot . . . only one name was mentioned. We rarely agree unanimously on anything, but a boat like the Hawk only comes around as often as a day when the Atlantic is smooth enough for barefooting.

OFFSHORE BOAT OF THE YEAR

EXCALIBUR 40' HAWK

With its price tag only pocket change away from $100,000, you expect the Excalibur to be something out of the ordinary. You can't appreciate just how special this boat is until you compare it side by side with the no-slouch megabucks rigs from the big guys. Concentrating on workmanship, styling, attention to detail and improved interior design, Excalibur President Bill Farmer doesn't claim to have the ultimate in performance with his new 40-footer, just the classiest rig on the water bar none. We agree.

Actually, the Hawk and the Chris-Craft 390X Stinger that we're recognizing for its Outstanding Quality of Workmanship are sisterships. But when it comes to assembling the bare hull, Farmer has the upper hand. Perhaps the most impressive feature of the Hawk is the seating arrangement in the first cabin. While most builders use a standard face-to-face couch in the entry cabin, Excalibur has designed an octagonal couch that can be made into a round bed with additional cushions. In the forward compartment there are sleeping accommodations for two more adults, and all of the interior upholstery work is done with top-grade materials.

Aiming to make your journey as comfortable as possible, Excalibur equips the Hawk with a good amount of storage space, a force-fed air ventilation system and a professional quality sound system. Our test machine didn't have a complete galley, but who cares? You rarely need more than an ice chest for most excursions, anyway. As a custom builder, Farmer designs the cabin to customer specifications, so if you want additional galley options they can be added.

Sometimes we go out on a limb, but we think this one's pretty sturdy: The Excalibur Hawk is the finest offshore machine ever produced.

Just Another Bend in the Road

BEFORE I LEAVE THE STORY OF THE CAREER THE Lord gave me, I'd like to tell you about two of the other businesses I had the privilege to invest in by His generous hand—boating and banking.

I have always loved cars and boats. If it had a big motor, then I was counted in! Through the years I owned a lot of great cars, Rolls Royces, Bentleys and Ferraris, and fast powerboats. Cars and boats were more than transportation to me; they were a serious hobby and added a lot of fun and freedom in the stresses of life.

In 1977, I purchased controlling interest in a speed boat manufacturing company called Excalibur Marine, located in Sarasota, Florida. I was lucky to have two great partners in the boat business, Bill Farmer and Don Abel, who knew the business well and could be trusted. They are still best friends of mine today.

Purchasing Excalibur Marine was more of a labor of love

Don Abel, Me and Bill Farmer

than a business for profit at the outset. The business was in trouble when I bought in. Thankfully, over the next seven years, I learned a lot and together we turned the company around. We won the world racing championship for two years, the production class, and were awarded "Boat of the Year" in 1981 and 1982.

Still and all, boat racing is a risky business. Unfortunately, our race boat driver was killed while testing one of our boats. I tried racing once in one of them and thought my head and neck would break off from the pounding! That was the last of *my* racing days.

Meanwhile, we expanded our line of boats, purchased a new plant, and invested a lot of time and money into the business. Just as we thought the business was becoming successful, interest rates under President Jimmy Carter jumped to 21 percent in 1983 and the country was in a recession. We could not sell a thing!

One afternoon as I was talking to my lawyer and accountant in my office about how to save the business, I received a phone call from the president of Wellcraft Marine. He asked me if I would be interested in selling the company; Excalibur was a great brand name in the boating world. I was in disbelief! I cannot thank God enough for always being there when I needed him. The Lord had come to my rescue once again at the eleventh hour! We sat there in amazement at God's goodness. I sold the business that next Monday morning! Now as I write my story, I still enjoy boating for pleasure but not for trying to make money.

Banking was another business in which I became involved. In 1986, Lou Katz, a lawyer friend of mine who lived nearby, asked me if I wanted to invest in a troubled bank with him and a few others in Cherry Hill, New Jersey. I accepted his offer. Together we invested millions of dollars in new capital in this bank called Cherry Hill Community Bank. After a short time, I learned the banking business and became chairman of the board! My experience in McDonald's retailing and management came in handy for this new venture. We turned this bank around and after five years, sold it to a big bank in Philadelphia, Pennsylvania at a nice profit. Thank God, we did very well with this investment.

During this time in banking, I met Dan Tabas who owned a bank in Philadelphia and we became good friends. Once we sold Cherry Hill Community Bank in 1990, Dan asked me to become a director of his bank, Royal Bank of America. I retired as a director of this bank in 2012.

Serving as a bank director has been a great learning experience. I have met a lot of wonderful people along the way. Out of my entire tenure as a director, these past five years from 2007 to 2012, have been the hardest for banks and the country since the Great Depression in 1929. After losing over $100 million dollars in bad real estate loans, it looks like the bank will be starting to return to profitability. This has been the ultimate turnaround experience and has taught me a lot about risk management.

These businesses were part-time for me, along with my full-time job running the McDonald's stores. To say the least, I kept myself quite busy! I want to praise God for seeing me through my life in many ways, both spiritual and temporal.

Sing Glory
The Lord has Done Wonderful Things

NOW I WANT TO TELL YOU MORE ABOUT THE wonderful things God has done for me and share the spiritual experiences He has given me on the road to becoming and being a minister in the Church of Jesus Christ. As you'll see, the Lord was good to me in spite of my many mistakes. Through it all, I never forgot the Lord and tried my best to serve Him, but truly all the praise and glory go to Him.

Come Sit with Us

GOING BACK TO 1968, I WAS DRIVING AND FELT A severe pain in my stomach, which became unbearable, so I drove to a nearby hospital for help. As I walked into the hospital, a voice spoke to me and said, "You do not have to be here," and the pain immediately left me. I started to praise God for his goodness and mercy. I was overcome with the relief from the pain that had been so severe. Driving home, I continued to thank God for this second miracle of healing in my life.

When I arrived home, I continued to praise and thank God. As I was lying in my bed praying, my body was lifted from the bed like an elevator. The speed that I felt as I was lifted into the air was unbelievable. The next thing I saw were two brothers flying alongside me in the air, Brother Matthew Rogolino and Brother Augie D'Orazio, who were ministers in the Gospel. I called out to them and said, "Where are we going?" They said to me, "Follow us." I saw the inside of the Edison Church. The Brothers then pointed down to the Rostrum bench of the Church and said, "Come sit with us." I then was back on my bed, just as quickly as I had left it, praising God for this experience. At the time I did not fully understand the purpose of this experience, but I do now. This experience 43 years before came to pass in 2011 when I was ordained a minister in the true Church of Jesus Christ.

Many events took place in my life in the years following this experience that I am *not* happy about. At times I let the things of this world interfere with my service to God and I made some poor choices and felt the consequences of those choices. Still, I never forgot the words of my father. He would say to me, "Remember the words in the Scriptures where it says that the Lord will bless you as long as you keep his commandments. If not, he will remove his presence from you." These words kept bringing me back when I left the straight and narrow way.

Edison Church

Unless the Lord Builds the House—

WHEN WE MOVED BACK TO THE SOUTHERN NEW Jersey area in 1971 to focus on the Philadelphia area McDonald's stores, we attended a small mission of the Church in Levittown (Fairless Hills), Pennsylvania. Brother Sam Dell was holding meetings in his home. We attended Church there and supported the Church in many ways. After a few years, the mission in Levittown started to grow. Working together with the Brothers and Sisters, we gave the seed money and support to build a new Church building. It was a joy and a labor of love for all of us to participate in the construction of this building. Today Levittown is a thriving branch of the Church. We experienced many blessings during our time as members of the Levittown branch. My wife, Lydia; her dear friend, Max Haufe (her mother's companion); and my daughters, Linda, Wendy Ann, and Alexis, and Alexis' mother were all baptized while we attended service there.

In 1975 while we attended services in Levittown, Sister Darlene Large asked to speak to me. She said that she had a dream where she was told that she would be involved with helping the Indian people. It was a powerful dream. At first she thought it was with the American Indians, but the Lord led her to understand that it was work in the country of India. Through another experience, Sister Darlene was also made to understand the name of the work should be called HOINA, or "HOMES OF THE INDIAN NATION." (www.HOINA.org)

Like any new venture, money was needed to get started. Sister Darlene asked me if I would invest the money they had put together to start this new work. I agreed. I am happy to say that the Lord blessed the investments that I made for them three-fold and this money then was used to start this wonderful work. The following is a letter to me from Sister Darlene when we were about to invest the seed money for the Lord.

Dear Brother Tony,

Well, finally, here it is; God bless and guide you with this money. You are not responsible for this money, as you said. Bruce and I are agreed on this point. We know you will do your best and that's all anyone can ask of anyone else. If you need a name, do it in the name of HOINA. It's God's money for his purpose. Gosh, I'm excited, my first business venture for HOINA. I wonder what will happen. God bless you. Our board members are me, Bruce, Brother Spencer Everett, Brother Joe Melatoni and Brother Pat Marinetti. India is so far away. I can hardly wait to see my other daughter there. Excuse this note but I'm so excited I'm going to burst. God is so wonderful. Brother Tony, thank you. May the Lord continue to bless you and may he grant you the desires of your heart.

Fondly,
Sister Darlene

Levittown Church

*My Father, Mother, Wendy Ann and Church Members
When Building was Dedicated in Levittown, PA*

Thirty-seven years later HOINA is a wonderful work with hundreds of homeless children being cared for and educated in the land of India. More importantly, the children are taught about Jesus Christ. The Lord has really blessed Sister Darlene in this work and I praise God that he put me in a position that I could be used by Him for helping start HOINA.

> Home of the Indian Nations
> **HOINA**
> Hope to the Orphaned
>
> March 10, 1975
>
> Dear Bro. Tony,
>
> Well — finally — here it is! God bless you and guide you. You are not responsible for this money, as you said. Bruce and I are agreed on this point. We know you'll do your best and that's all anyone can ask of anyone else.
>
> If you need a name, do it in the name of <u>HOINA</u>. It's God's money for his purposes.
>
> Gosh, I'm excited. My first business venture for Hoina. I wonder what will happen?
>
> God bless you. Our board members are me, Bruce, Bro. Spencer Everett, Bro. Joe Milantoni and Bro. Pat Marinette.
>
> India is so far. I can hardly wait to see my other daughter.
>
> Excuse this note but I'm so excited I'm going to burst. God is so wonderful.
>
> Bro. Tony, thank you. May the Lord continue to bless you and may He grant you the desires of your heart. Fondly,
>
> P.S. To.. Bruce, Jr.: Love. Sis. Darlene

Dear Brother Tony,
  Today one of our boys asked me to tell them the story of Hoima. I told them about how it all happened and about the part you played in it. It really is quite a story. Thousands of kids have been rescued. I'm writing to all our donors to thank them. I've had some arrythmia problems of the heart and at 73½ I'm not sure how much longer I will be here. So – thank you for all your help. You've fed a lot of orphans and widows. God bless you. You've fed a lot of Americans too. I wanted to do something special for your family so I bought a section of fence for Wendy and Bro. Sam Dell.

The "HONORS" fence really looks nice. I wish you & your family could see it. It's been there since last year. I felt so bad when she was taken so soon from the earth.
  Bruce has been doing a lot of work in Africa.

*You have a spirit of kindness
that sets you apart...
There's hope for the world
in people like you.*

He loves the people. He's been to 6 countries. This year he spent 2 months there.
  Letti & Todd are well and Dirk is a lot better. He's lost 70 lbs. His diabetes caused him to lose 9 molars to an infection.

Supporting the Church in Tampa, Florida

BACK IN 1975 WE STARTED TRAVELING TO Florida in the winter and attended a small mission in Tampa, Florida. Brother Billy Tucker was holding meetings with a few members. As in Levittown, we felt the blessings of the Lord in our meetings and the mission started to grow. I made the decision to fund and purchase a small Church building in Tampa, Florida. In just a few years, the Lord continued to bless us and the Church grew in membership. Over time we outgrew the building in Tampa and the members decided to separate and build a new branch in nearby Forest Hills, where many members lived. Eventually, the two branches joined together in Forest Hills. The Tampa branch building was sold some years later for eight times what I paid for it. From just a few members in Tampa, Florida in the 1970s, today in 2012 the branch in Forest Hills is blessed with almost a hundred members and is looking again to expand to a larger building. My mother in-law, who has since passed away from cancer on January 9, 2010, was baptized in the Forest Hills branch on February 18, 2007. It has been quite a blessing to my family and me to have been involved in helping souls come to God and helping the Church grow in Florida.

I Will Never Leave You or Forsake You

EARLIER IN MY STORY, I SHARED THAT AFTER MY first divorce in 1978 I was not able to be a full member in the Church for sixteen years, but I continued to attend faithfully. I took losing my membership very hard and many tears were shed for a long time. The last thing I ever wanted to do was displease the Lord. I thank God for the Brothers and Sisters who supported and encouraged me. I received many phone calls and cards during this time when I was really depressed. I saved all the cards and one day, years later, I started reading them. I opened a letter from Brother Cleve Baldwin from Quincy, Florida, who was a good friend of my father and our family. As I read his words of encouragement, I felt the need to send him five hundred dollars for the Church in Quincy, Florida, and thank him again for his support during those times when I really needed it. A few weeks later, I received a letter back from him. He wrote, "Brother Tony, I want you to know that when we received your check the Church was broke. We had answered the call of the General Church for needed funds and gave them $500 dollars, which was all we had. Then your check came that day and replaced it! God saw our need and touched your heart." I am always amazed at how God works. This was a wonderful experience for us all to remember.

A Nigerian Home in Memory of My Mother and Father

AS THE YEARS PASSED, I WANTED TO HONOR MY FAther and mother in some way for all they had done for us in our lives. In the 1980s, Brother Joe Ross wrote me a letter asking me for monetary help in the missionary work in Nigeria, Africa. The Church had started an orphanage for homeless children there and they needed funding. I agreed to support the orphanage and asked him for a favor as well. I asked Brother Joe Ross if he would put a cornerstone on the front of the building honoring my parents. He agreed and the orphanage stands as a memorial for my parents and a home for the children with no place to go. We could never repay my parents for everything they did for us. They risked all the money

they had to start an uncertain business venture with McDonald's and they taught me about the Gospel of Jesus Christ.

THE
CHURCH OF JESUS CHRIST
In the United States of America

HEADQUARTERS
SIXTH & LINCOLN ST.
MONONGAHELA, PA 15063

JOSEPH ROSS
#2 ROSS DRIVE
ALIQUIPPA, PA 15001
PHONE 412-375-1648

<u>FOREIGN MISSIONS OPERATING COMMITTEE</u>

December 26, 1996

Dear Tony & Nancy:

I trust this short note finds you and your children well, still enjoying the Holiday Season, and enjoying God's richest blessings. As for us, we are well, thank God.

Enclosed find the promised photographs of the plaque installed on the main entrance to the Orphanage in Nigeria, and a front view photo of the building. You can see the plaque is in a prominent location as it should be. We have named the facility a Social Welfare building that houses accomodations for orphans, classrooms for instructing the orphans and neighboring children, a minature clinic to care for the orphans, a chapel for the local Abak Church congregation, living quarters for the matron, instructors, security guards, and offices for those in charge of the center.

We are in the process of renovating, painting, purchasing beds, desks, etc. for the hopeful dedication in early February or Spring of 1997. They want to plan the ceremony when our missionaries from the U.S. are there. Of course, you both know that you are invited to be guests of honor for that ceremony. I wrote and told them that decision would be yours, however, I did explain to them how busy you are in business. So I sort of left the door open for you. Once the renovations are completed they will send more photos which I will send to you both. Again, in behalf of those orphans, we thank you for providing a home for them. May God bless and reward you a hundredfold.

Yours in Christ, African Missions Coordinators

Joseph Perri   Joseph Ross

The Joy of Being Used to Fill a Need

THE LORD HAS ALWAYS FOUND A WAY TO USE ME TO help the Church and its members, for which I am grateful. I remember visiting a few of the branches of the Church in New Jersey and Brooklyn, New York. While visiting these older buildings of the church, I noticed the bathrooms were really in terrible condition. I decided to donate the monies to rebuild these bathrooms, which were badly needed. I became tagged with the nickname "The Bathroom Brother."

In the 1980s Brother Nathan Peterkin, a minister in the Edison (New Jersey) branch who was a good friend of my father, retired from work. He wanted to go back to his home town of Spartanburg, North Carolina, and preach the Gospel to his friends there, so he moved his family south. The Lord had blessed Brother Nathan with a tremendous speaking voice. After he was there for a while, Brother Nathan started a radio program on Sunday mornings. For many years, we assisted him in financing the radio program. Brother Nathan would send me letters and tapes of his sermons and tell me how every penny was accounted for. Eventually, after many years of hard work, the Lord gave him what he was working for—a congregation. He started out by building a small Church building in his backyard. I remember visiting him there. This dear and humble Brother said that he was amazed that "a man of my position" would take the time to come and visit him. My family and I were greatly blessed during that visit. Little did Brother Nathan realize that I felt no better than him. We were both servants of the Lord. Here is an excerpt of a letter Brother Nathan sent me in 1987 that I will always cherish, since he has now gone home to be with the Lord.

> Dear Brother Tony,
>
> It's a great pleasure to sit here tonight to write a few lines to let you know how we are doing. I hope when this letter reaches you, it will find you and your family well. My family is doing fine, but I am still struggling, trying to make it. I've seen some very dark days since I've seen you, it looked as though I wasn't going to make it, but thank God I'm still around. [He suffered with lung problems from work] I certainly appreciate the check you have sent me this past week and the others you have sent this year. I am still broadcasting over the radio. It's costing me $220.00 every four weeks. I thank God I am able to pay it. With the help from you, I am able to pay more-so. You have been, and still are, a great help to this radio program. I have been broadcasting for seven years and nine months, I hope I can continue, if not I will step down. By the way, we are to baptize a young man this coming Saturday which will bring our membership to 14 members. Thank God I am not hungry, and the restored

Gospel is being preached here in the city of Spartanburg, North Carolina. I want to apologize for not writing you sooner than I have. Thank God for a Brother like you, tell your family the visit you made to our home here will never be forgotten or erased from my memory.

It is wonderful to see people, though they may be highly blessed of the Lord, yet they are able to share that love with common people. Not many people would do what you did, Brother Tony. Well, Brother Tony, this is about all I have to say this time. I hope by the help of God, that we all will prove faithful until the end of our days here on earth. Thanks again, a trillion times, for what you have done for this mission.

May God bless you.
Your Brother in Christ,
Brother Nathan Peterkin

Today a beautiful Church building stands for the glory of God in Spartanburg. Brother Nathan worked hard—he never gave up and his dream of a Church in his home town came to pass. I praise God I was able to help and be part of this work for the Lord.

I remember in the same time period that Brother Apostle Joe Calabrese began a work in India. I assisted him financially over the years along with others. I remember the letters and conversations we had about the work in India with him and Doctor Livingston.

Thanks to the hard work of Brother Joe and many others today, India has hundreds of members and many Church buildings.

TADEPALLIGUDEM 534 101. India
22nd, JULY 1986.

MY BELOVED BROTHER ANTHONY MICALE,

    MY LOVING AND AFFECTIONATE AND HOLY KISSES TO YOU BOTH AND TO ALL OTHER SAINTS THERE.

    I HAVE RECEIVED YOUR LOVING LETTER DATED 8th, JULY '86 JUST TO-DAY AND MY LIPS ARE FILLED PRAISE AND THANKS GIVING TO OUR ALMIGHTY LORD WHO IS ALWAYS FAITHFUL TO HIS CHILDREN WHO BELIEVE IN HIM AND DEPEND UPON HIM FOR ALL THE SPIRITUAL AND ALSO FOR THEIR NATURAL NEEDS.MAY HE BE GLORIFIED IN AND THROUGH ME DURING ALL THE REST OF TIME UNTIL WE MEET HIM FACE TO FACE.

    I THANK YOU VERY MUCH FOR THIS LOVING GIFT OF YOURS THAT YOU SO LOVINGLY ARE SENDING THROUGH MY BOSS, BROTHER JOE CALABRESE TO HELP ME IN MY HOSPITAL EXPENCES FOR SURGERY FOR MY SON SOLOMON WHO IS ALSO A BAPTISED MEMEBR OF OUR CHURCH HERE.HE WAS BAPTISED BY BROTHER JOE WHEN HE BAPTISED ME ON THE DECEMBER 6th,1981.OUR LORD JESUS CHRIST WILL FILL YOU WITH HIS SPIRIT AND MAY HE BE GLORIFIED AND MAY HE FILL YOU WITH HEAVENLY BLESSINGS FOR THIS ACT OF KINDNESS SHOWN TOWARDS MY NEEDY SON AND WE ALL LIFT YOU ALL UP AT THE THRONE OF GRACE FOR YOUR DUE HEAVENLY REWARD.

    HOPING TO HEAR FROM YOU AS AND WHEN THE SPIRIT LEADS;KISSES FROM YOUR 4 FOSTER CHILDREN WHO WILL DEVELOP TO BE FUTURE PILLARS OF THE CHURCH OF JESUS CHRIST;

    EVER PRAYING FOR YOU AND FOR ALL THE OTHER SAINTS THERE;KINDLY DO PRAY FOR OUR SPIRITUAL AND ALSO FOR OUR NATURAL NEEDS; WITH MY LOVING KISSES TO YOU MY BELOVED BROTHER,

    YOURS IN THE SOUL-WINNING MINISTRY,

(B.D.LIVINGSTON)

Brother, B.D LIVINGSTON
ELDER
The Church of Jesus Christ
TADEPALLIGUDEM - 534 101,
Andhra Pradesh S. India

Another important event occurred in the 1990s. The Church was deep in debt. Brother Apostle Paul Benyola, who was a financial banking expert, came up with the idea of starting a Humanitarian Fund for the Church to get the Church out of debt. I am happy to say that the Lord used me to give Brother Paul the seed money it needed to start this fund. Today this fund is called the Humanitarian Foundation Fund (HFF) and the Church is out of debt. Most amazing is that the Church has the ability to finance itself. This has been a great blessing to the Church.

I thank God that in 1994 through the efforts of the Church Apostles and leadership of the Church, the laws were changed. Brother Paul Benyola was a key supporter of the change, which allowed forgiveness for divorce and reinstatement of Church membership, if you were truly repentant. I once again became a full member of the Church of Jesus Christ, for which I praise God.

The Lord is My Strength

An Amazing Story of God's Rescue

IN 2002, THE LORD CAME TO MY RESCUE ONCE again when I almost lost my life in a boating accident on the New Jersey shore. That summer the Army Corps of Engineers dredged an inlet near our home and rogue waves had overtaken many boaters, drowning them due to broken bones suffered in the impact. I was boating with a few friends, going full throttle in this inlet, when a rogue wave hit us. The impact was so severe that my boat went straight up in the air like a rocket. I knew we had been hit hard, but thank God, everyone was still in the boat. We knew that some of my passengers had broken bones, but one of them was able to use his cell phone and dial 911 so that the paramedics would meet us back at the boat dock. I didn't realize it at the time, but my boat was totaled and I had severely broken my leg and hip and was losing blood at a staggering rate. Although my leg and hip were literally smashed to pieces, God gave me the strength to drive that boat back to our home dock.

Paramedics were waiting there for us. I was taken to Shore Memorial Hospital in Ocean City, because they didn't think I would make it all the way back to Philadelphia. Little did I know that God was directing everything. When I arrived at the hospital, the surgeon on duty "happened" to have been the son of our next-door neighbor back in Vestal, New York. Our kids had played together! To our surprise, this young man had grown up to be a leading orthopedic trauma surgeon in Philadelphia. He looked at my chart and realized who he was about to treat—I learned later that this young surgeon had looked up to me when he was a boy and thought of me as a role model! What are the chances that I would have such a specially-trained physician who knew me personally and cared for my welfare? I am convinced that this amazing turn of events was only by the hand of God.

Still, my prognosis was not good. The doctor thought I was going to die that night, since I had lost eight pints of blood and my leg was in pieces. I remember my wife, Lydia, calling Brother Paul Benyola, who dropped everything and drove to the hospital to anoint me. Despite the extreme loss of blood and the doctors' consternation about where it was coming from, the Lord kept me alive.

I also learned later that my daughter, Linda, living in California at that time, awoke from a nightmare a few nights before my accident. She was screaming out loud, because she saw me in a "car" underwater, drowning and unable to get to the surface. Her roommate, Carolyn, came running to find out what was wrong, and when Linda told her, Carolyn immediately said, "Let's pray for the Lord to protect your dad." And they did—never knowing until a few days later what that prayer of protection was meant for. As it turned out, my boat was the only boat hit by rogue waves in the inlet that summer that had ANY survivors.

After months of slow recovery, I lived to praise God once more. There is a steel rod in my leg and hip now that they used to put my leg back together. I have always felt that the Lord spared my life for a reason; He had work for me to do and He is good.

Building a Branch of the Church in South Jersey

The Lord's Timing

WE WORSHIPED IN LEVITTOWN UNTIL 2005 WHEN the members who lived in south Jersey decided to start a new branch of the Church in Mt. Laurel. In the beginning, we held meetings in a school. Then in order to save money, we moved to an empty office space in one of my office buildings in New Jersey. After a few years of planning, we began the project. This is the story of how the Lord provided funds for building the branch—in his perfect timing.

A year before, in 2004, we put our house in Longport, New Jersey, on the market. The real estate market was "hot" and we were sure that this beautiful property would sell quickly. Oddly enough, it didn't! Everything around us was selling and we just couldn't figure out what was going on. Lydia and I told one another that one day we would look back and know the reason the house didn't sell. One and a half years later, in 2005, the house finally sold.

Mt. Laurel, New Jersey Branch Church

When it did sell, it was around the same time we were considering building a new Church in Mt. Laurel. Driving home from the sale, I wondered to myself, "Where am I going to invest this money?" At that very moment, the Lord spoke to my heart: "Take part of this money and build the Church in Mt. Laurel." In the next second I thought, "Oh my goodness! The Lord had a time in mind when we needed to buy the land and He put off the sale of the house to the point where we had the money to help pay for the Church at the right time!"

As a result of that sale, my family was able to commit half the cost of the project. By God's perfect timing and matchless grace, today a beautiful new Church stands in Mt. Laurel, New Jersey, for the honor and glory of God and the community.

The Beginning of Our Family's Work in Italy

THE NEXT SPIRITUAL TURNING POINT WAS IN 2005, when I was sitting at Bob Evans for breakfast during a spring Church conference in Pennsylvania. Brother John Di Battista came over to our table and starting talking to us. I said, "I heard you are having a conference in Italy in September and we would like to attend. I have had a strong desire to go, since I heard about it." Brother John said, "Please come, we are looking for all the help and support we can get." Brother John was chairman of the International Missionary Operating Committee (IMOC) at the time. He later told me he was prompted to come to our table by the Lord. I cannot say enough about the love and support I have received from Brother John Di Battista, Brother Alex Gentile and Brother Apostle Paul Benyola in the years since. After that first trip to Italy, Lydia and I were hooked. Remember that I told you that Lydia speaks fluent Italian? How the Lord works! What could be more perfect for missionaries

San DeMetrio, Italy
Branch of the Church

to Italy? The Lord filled us with so many experiences and blessings, there was no turning back. Before I share more about Italy, there is another part of this road with the Lord that I need to tell about.

Wendy Ann Goes Home

EARLY THE NEXT YEAR, WE EXPERIENCED A DEVAStating time, the loss of my daughter, Wendy Ann. She died suddenly in February 2006 from a heart valve problem; she was only 46 when she passed. Wendy Ann was living in Florida with her mother, Marie, who found her. Losing a child is one of the hardest things any parent can go through. It was devastating for our family. A great comfort to us was when her mother found her that morning in bed, the Scriptures were open next to her on the bed. She had been reading God's word—the Book of Matthew—before she died.

We *know* she is with the Lord. Her sister, Linda, said that a few weeks before Wendy Ann passed away, the Lord kept bringing Scriptures to mind about 'a treasure in heaven'. Linda said that she would hear this over and over on radio broadcasts and in passages she was reading in a Bible study that year. She told her husband, Jeff, about this and he responded, "The Lord must be preparing you for a loss." They wondered what it

Wendy Ann Micale at 8 months old

Wendy Ann and Linda

Wendy Ann at 2 years old

Father and Daughter

could be. A week or so later, Jeff's stepfather passed away. He was a wonderful man of God. Linda and Jeff thought that this still couldn't be what the verses were about. The very next day, Linda heard another radio sermon about treasure in heaven from a pastor who had lost his daughter. He was crying out to God about her death, but felt the Lord comforting him—"You have a treasure in heaven and it is your daughter." Immediately, Linda knew this was what the verses were about, but she still didn't know why she was receiving them. That Sunday morning, Wendy Ann died and Linda knew without a doubt that the Lord had been preparing her for this terrible day. It was another comfort at a time when comfort was hard to find. We praise God that because of His kindness, we know that Wendy Ann is with Him in heaven.

Lisa J. Sowers
1340 Brookhaven Circle NE
Atlanta, GA 30319
(404) 429-0059
Email: ljsowers@comcast.net

April 24, 2006

Mr. Anthony Micale
1121 Winding Drive PO Box 2680
Cherry Hill, N.J. 08003

Dear Mr. Micale:

I don't know if you remember me, as it has been approximately fourteen years, but I was friends with your daughter Wendy when I lived in Collingswood, New Jersey, from 1990 to 1991. Wendy brought me to your house in Cherry Hill a couple of times, and on one occasion, I had dinner with you, Wendy, and your wife Nancy. To refresh your memory, Wendy and I worked together on various paralegal assignments in Philadelphia, and were friends for a couple of years. I went away to law school in Michigan in 1992. Shortly after that, I got very busy, transferred to a law school in Atlanta, Georgia, and Wendy and I lost touch. Regrettably, I lost touch not just with Wendy, but with many of my friends up North.

Many years have gone by since then, but this past week, for whatever reason, I couldn't get Wendy out of my mind. I became so preoccupied with her, that I decided to look her up on the internet, and see if I could track her down. It was then that I came upon the very sad news about her passing in February 2006. Let me begin this letter by expressing my deepest sympathies to both you and your family. I am so terribly sorry for your loss. I can't imagine how difficult this must be for you.

I don't know if you are aware of this, but for the couple of years that Wendy and I were close, we had many conversations about different topics. Without betraying any confidences, what stands out most was how frequently you were the focus of those conversations. I can tell you this much - at least at that time - Wendy's relationship with you was the most significant relationship of her life.

In fact, it appeared to me that the most important thing in this world to her was that she would be able to make you proud of her. She was in awe of you and your accomplishments. I sometimes got the impression that she didn't know if she could ever match them. So the focus of her time was spent on working very hard - harder, that is, than most people I know, to be as good as she possibly could be in every way possible, so that you would be proud of her. I was glad to see (I found this out also on the internet also at www.ancestry.com.) that Wendy did go to law school on a part time basis, as I know that was one of her goals.

Obviously when one passes at the age of 46, it is very premature. Had she been ill? I don't want to pry, but I deeply regret not getting in touch with her much sooner. Wendy was there for me in some very difficult times, and I wish that I could have been there for her.

Did Wendy have a favorite charity? Is there anything I can do in her memory? Perhaps make a donation to that charity in her name? I have included my contact information at the top of this letter. Please feel free to use it.

A letter I received from a friend of Wendy Ann.

A Blessing Even in a Time of Sorrow

As I have written, as a result of Wendy Ann's passing, the year 2006 was one of the hardest our family has experienced. The whole family came together at our home in Cherry Hill for Christmas that year, and we put a special angel on the tree to remember Wendy Ann. On Christmas morning, I awoke from sleep around 5:00 A.M. I could not go back to sleep and this was very unusual for me. I decided to get up and make a pot of coffee and read some Scripture.

As I was waiting for the coffee to brew, I noticed a copy of *Missionary News* on the table. Since I had just started to join the work in Italy, I read the newsletter. There was one small article in the newsletter about the Philippines. This was new work and they desperately needed two buildings where they could worship in the villages of Sierra Bullones, Bohol, Philippines. As I was reading this, the Lord touched my heart. I emailed Brother John Di Battista, Chair of the IMOC for the Church, and wrote: "Tell Brother Art Gehly, Sr. (who was leading the work there) that they will have their two buildings. Sister Lydia and I will pledge the monies needed." Now I knew why I could not sleep. The Lord was prompting me to help in the Philippines work. I went into the bedroom with tears in my eyes and woke up my wife, Lydia, and told her the experience I just had. The Lord woke me up and stopped me from sleeping so I would read this article and come to their aid. Today there are at least two beautiful Church buildings in the Philippines. I cannot thank God enough for allowing me the privilege to help build his Kingdom on earth.

Church in the Philippines

The Lord Answers Prayers in Italy

THE LORD HAS PLACED A PASSION FOR ITALY ON MY heart so that people there would know Him and that the Church there would grow and be encouraged. The following are a few of the experiences we have had there.

On our first trip to Italy we traveled to the island of Sardinia for the Church conference. The first stop we made was at Sister Immaculata's house. She was an anchor in the Church in Italy. She and her husband, who has since passed away, built the Church in Sardinia. She was 80 years old and had just been sent home from the hospital with a stroke and a broken back. She was not expected to live. When I entered her house, I was drawn to visit her. Her granddaughters who understand English were with her in her bedroom. I introduced myself to them and sat down on the bed next to Sister Immaculata. I felt such compassion for her.

Then I held her hand and started to talk to her. I told her that the Lord would not forget her. As I was encouraging her,

Church in Sardinia, Italy

the Spirit of God came upon me very strongly. I started to cry as I continued to tell her the Lord would take care of her. We all felt the Spirit of God there that day. It is something I will never forget. This was the first of many blessings and experiences we have received in Italy.

I returned the next day and the same thing happened again as I continued to encourage her and tried to uplift her. The following day, Brother Apostle Joe Lovalvo came to join us and prayed for her also. Then on the third day, Sister Immaculata was sitting upright in her chair. She recovered and lived another six years to the amazement of everyone in town! The Lord had let me know while I was praying that He was going to heal her.

A few days after our visits with Sister Immaculata, we met a young lady named Stefania. During a testimony meeting at the Church in Sardinia, Stefania, who had not yet joined the

Church, was giving an experience she had that the Lord told her she was accepted by Him. As she said this, the Spirit of the Lord said to me, "Ask her if she feels she is accepted by God, then as Alma says in the Scripture at the waters of Mormon, if you feel this way, what is stopping you then from being baptized in the Church and making a covenant with him?" I stood up and said these words. The Spirit of the Lord fell on all of us and the tears started to flow as she sat down. She asked where this is found in the Scriptures. We showed her and she sat down, reading the words of Alma. After the service, she gave me back the Book of Mormon and thanked me.

Another blessing at this conference was that Apostle Brother Joe Lovalvo was in attendance. This was his last missionary trip before he died at 96 years old. Brother Joe and I spent a lot of time together, which really was a joy to me. He just loved to talk about experiences. That night we were eating ice cream and talking. The Brothers found us and asked if we had heard the news. We said we hadn't and they told us that Stefania wanted to be baptized. She said to them that what Brother Tony said was from God. It is hard to describe the joy we all felt that night. These two experiences happened on our first trip to Italy. The next day she entered into the water and salvation was found in her life.

The Enemy Prowls Around Like a Roaring Lion

WE ALSO KNOW THAT THE ENEMY OF OUR SOUL IS not happy with us when we labor for the Lord. Three different times I have had dreams that scared me almost to death. The first time was in San Demetrio with Brother Alex Gentile. We had decided to rebuild the Church building, which was in very bad repair. I agreed to fund the cost of the repairs, including building a one-bedroom apartment for missionaries to use. That night I was visited by the enemy of my soul coming at me in a dream. His face was terrible and ugly—I had never felt such fear in all my life. I cried out to the Lord and the devil left me. He was not happy that we were going to rebuild the Church.

The second time we were at a conference in Greensburg, Pennsylvania. My wife and I were talking to Brother Joe Benyola in the lobby about the blessings we had received in missionary work. Brother Joe said to me, be careful, when you are receiving these blessings—the enemy is not happy. I made the mistake of saying, "I am not worried about it." That night my wife and stepdaughter, Chiara, went to our room and stayed up watching television; I fell asleep. Again I had a dream as I did before in Italy. I was in a dark room and I could feel the presence of evil in the room. I then saw a personage coming at me with the most horrible face with teeth like a lion. The fear that came over me was indescribable! I could not speak; I tried to cry out to the Lord but could not.

While I was experiencing this great fear, Lydia and Chiara saw what was happening to me. They said my eyes rolled back, my face became distorted and they heard me trying to call out. They tried to wake me up, but could not. Finally, I cried out the name of the Lord with all my strength and the evil one left me and I awoke. My family looked at me in shock and disbelief. I tried to explain what had just happened to me.

The third time this happened to me, the dream was similar, except the devil was dressed well and good-looking but the fear I felt was the same. This leads us to know that the enemy of our soul can come at us in many forms. I told Brother John Di Battista about this dream. He said to me that he and Brother Alex saw this same person in San Demetrio staring at them the last time they were there.

More of God's Blessings in Italy

THE FOLLOWING IS AN EXPERIENCE WE HAD IN Cala Gonone, Sardinia, while on a missionary trip there. This experience was printed in the *Gospel News*.

After visiting the saints, holding meetings and working with the contractor who was remodeling the building in San Demetrio, Calabria, we left the mainland and went by overnight ferry to the island of Sardinia. Upon our arrival there, our young Sister Stefania asked us if we would anoint her friend, Antonella, who had cancer. We made arrangements to have her come to Brother Rosario's home where several of us had gathered. When Antonella arrived, she explained her condition and we could see the bandages on her right shoulder where the cancerous tumor was located. The fear on her face spoke volumes and no further questions were needed.

We explained to her the ordinances of laying on of hands for the sick. She seemed comfortable with us and we all knelt in prayer. As we were on our knees, I began silently praying that this young woman would receive a miracle like the people of old did whenever they came in contact with Jesus. After a season of prayer on our knees, the ministry attended to the laying on of hands. The lot fell on Brother John Di Battista and he began praying. Brother John states that there was no doubt in his mind that the words he spoke were not his. The Spirit was strong and we all said goodbye with hugs and kisses.

It was then that I relayed the following experience. I said that the words spoken by Brother John were the exact words that I prayed silently while we on our knees before his prayer. The Spirit of God was in that room. This was a beautiful confirmation and blessing of our service to God.

It Will Not Harm Them

THREE MONTHS LATER WHEN WE GATHERED IN Rome for our annual conference (in 2007), we received the report that the cancer was not altogether gone in Antonella. Sister Stefania asked that we anoint a handkerchief for her. We read in the Bible that when someone is sick and an Elder cannot come that they anointed a handkerchief with oil and prayed that when the person receiving it put it on the affected part of the body, the Lord would heal her if she had faith. The Book of Acts 19:11-12a says: "And God wrought special miracles by the hands of Paul: So that from his body were brought unto the sick handkerchiefs or aprons, and the diseases departed from them..." As we prayed, the power of God attended us once again. We felt the fire of the Holy Spirit fill the handkerchief we had prayed on for her. Stefania gave the cloth to Antonella who wore it on the spot where the cancerous tumor was found. We are happy to report that Antonella is now cancer-free and is expecting her second child. The next time we visited Sardinia, she came to greet us. What a joy

MY LIFE EXPERIENCES ON THE ROAD...

Brother Giovanni Marino, Presiding Elder in Italy, Evangelist John DiBattista, Evangelist Alex Gentile and Brother Rosario Scravaglieri, the President of The Church of Jesus Christ in Italy

we saw on her face and what a boost to the faith for our small mission on the Island of Sardinia. We are thankful to God for the witness of our young Sister Stefania and her desire to see others come to know the Church of Jesus Christ.

A few years ago in 2009, I had another experience while we were in San Demetrio, Calabria, Italy on a missionary trip. We had just arrived and were having lunch. Brother John Di Battista, his wife, Caryl, and I had planned a three-week trip. While I was eating, I got a stain on my shirt. I left the table to call my wife, not thinking about the stain. While I was talking to her on the telephone, the restaurant owner put a small coke-shaped bottle in front of me. I thought to myself, "That's nice; she has given me a refreshing drink after dinner." I was so busy talking to my wife that I did not take the time to check out what was in the bottle. I picked up the bottle and swallowed a mouthful. I realized then that it was dry-cleaning fluid! When I looked further at the bottle, I saw the cross bone skeleton with the words, *poison*, written on it. They had given it to me to clean the stain off my shirt. I started coughing and choking. I was in disbelief of what just happened.

Lydia was listening to all this with alarm. She asked me, "Tony, what's wrong"? When I told her what had happened, she told to me go to the hospital, call a doctor. She was in a worse panic then I was! My first thoughts were to call the greatest doctor of all—the Lord Jesus Christ. The Lord put into my mind the last few verses in the Gospel of Mark. In short it says, "Go ye into the world and preach my gospel… And these signs that follow them that believe… if you drink any deadly thing it will not hurt you." (Mark 16:15-18) I asked Brother John to pray for me, and he did so in the middle of the hotel lobby. I had no fear, because I believed the words of our Savior. I knew He would take care of me, although as the day went on, I could still taste the poison in my mouth.

That evening I went to sleep and in the morning, I woke up soaking wet with blood on my pillow. The Lord had removed the poison from my body while I was sleeping. I praised God for His goodness and mercy and for keeping His word. We continued on the trip for the next few weeks enjoying God's blessings. The words in the Scriptures are true. When you work for the Lord, He is with you. I could fill pages with the experiences we all have had in the missionary field.

Come and See – The Lord's Work in Florida

I WAS ORDAINED AS A TEACHER IN 2007, AFTER two years in the missionary field in Italy. At that point, my involvement in the Church really started to fill my life, not only in Italy but in the domestic work in my local branches in Mt. Laurel, New Jersey, and in Cape Coral, Florida. As I wrote earlier, Sister Lydia and I worked together with the Brothers and Sisters in Mt. Laurel to help fund and build a new building for our growing congregation. This was a labor of love. After three years of planning and praying, a beautiful new branch of the Church was open, not only for us, but for the local community.

Then as presiding Teacher, I was able to grow and learn with the help of God and my elder Brother and Apostle, Paul Benyola. During this time, we would travel to Florida to our home in Sarasota and visit the Cape Coral Mission each month. Brother Skip Swanson presided over the mission and was alone most of the time. He put me to work each time I visited. This was also a wonderful learning experience for me. Brother Skip was a strong advocate for me and his support and help was greatly appreciated. Brother Skip and his sisters have opened their home to us many times as we traveled there for services.

About a year and a half after the Church building was completed in Mt. Laurel, I felt the Lord calling me to the work in Florida to help Brother Skip. It is hard to explain the feeling I had that my work was now in Cape Coral, Florida. We had been spending a lot of time in Florida because Lydia's mother, Coleen, was very ill with cancer. In fact, Sister Lydia and I had decided to move to Florida to care for her mother and become members in the Cape Coral mission.

I know the Lord was in the matter. We are working now in 2012 on a growth plan for the Cape Coral mission. In the past year, we have paved the road to the Church, painted the building and installed a road sign that says, "COME AND SEE." We

Evangelist John DiBattista baptizing Phil Brickhouse

Our Florida Home

The Cape Coral Church in Florida

also have just installed new landscaping and a sprinkler system. The Church needs to look bright and appealing to the community. We also have started to reach out to the community by handing out five hundred brochures explaining who we are and what we believe. Later this year, we plan to hold a large weekend event to introduce ourselves to the community.

Although our home in Florida is 77 miles from the Cape Coral Church, this does not stop us from giving our testimony to our friends and cousins living in Sarasota. We have had several wonderful experiences and events in our home.

During a missionary trip visit to Florida, Brothers John Di Battista and Joel Gehly, who headed the IMOC for the Church, were giving presentations of their many trips overseas working in the mission field. We invited as many friends and family members as we could to come to our home and hear these Brothers speak. I am happy to say that we had eighteen in attendance. The Spirit of God was felt by all. One of the people attending was my brother-in-law, Phil Brickhouse. During our Brothers' visit, Phil was touch by the Spirit of God. During dinner he asked, "How do I become like you Brothers? You are the kind of people I want to be with and be part of."

We gave our testimony and told him what the Lord says you have to do to be living in the Gospel. He said, "I want to be baptized." What a joy we all felt! On Mother's Day in May 2009, we all witnessed him being baptized in the waters behind our house in the Sarasota Bay. Every time we look out my backyard over the water, I think of that day. His mother, Coleen, was especially happy to see her son make his commitment to the Lord.

In Honor of Coleen, Lydia's Mother

THEN IN AUGUST OF 2009, WE HELD A SPECIAL Church service in our home for Coleen. She was very weak from cancer and could not make the trip to Cape Coral for services. It was actually Sister Linda Conger who gave us the idea to have this meeting in our home in Sarasota. She said, "If Coleen cannot come to us, we should come to Sarasota and hold a service for her!" We invited all our friends to the service. We had visiting ministers from Forest Hills, Brother Sam Risola, Brother Phil Benyola and others with their wives. Brother Skip Swanson came with members from Cape Coral, Florida. What a blessing we had that day—over 55 people attended that Church service in our home! We moved all the living room furniture out and Brother Skip brought in folding chairs that filled the room. The Spirit was strong and there was not a dry eye in the room. It was a blessing to us and to Coleen to see the love we all had for her and to worship the Lord in our home.

My mother-in-law, Coleen Brickhouse, was a wonderful

woman who loved the Lord and was an educator with an extraordinary vision for what children could become. She believed every child deserved the chance to learn and to be given the opportunity to succeed. She dedicated her life to the education and betterment of thousands of children and their families. Over the years, Coleen founded Brickhouse Academy, a private college preparatory school for children in Sarasota, Florida. It is recognized throughout the state for outstanding achievements in education. The school offers exceptional education and understanding to those struggling with learning disabilities and those who were extremely gifted and bright. After Coleen's passing, Lydia and I are happy to say that we took over the school and it is continuing to carry on the traditions of her mother. The school is blessed to have a wonderful teaching staff led by Allison Ditra, principal.

My mother-in-law, Coleen Brickhouse

Jesus Never Fails
On Becoming a Minister in the Church of Jesus Christ

NOW IT IS 2012. AFTER SIX YEARS, THIRTEEN TRIPS in the Italian work and four years as an ordained Teacher, I now have been called into the ministry. When I was first told by the Brothers that I was being recommended to the ministry of the Church, I felt the desires of my heart *being fulfilled*. I wanted to be able to work for the Lord with the ability to perform all the Church ordinances. As an ordained Teacher, my ability was limited. I desired this only for His honor and glory. The road of my entire life with Jesus Christ led up to this time.

Brother Scott Griffith and the regional officers of the Church asked me to fill out a questionnaire to consider my fitness for this ministry. There were many questions about my faith and beliefs. I felt this was very important because a minister of the Gospel must be in accord with the faith and doctrine of the Church. Once I filled out the questionnaire, the regional officers and Apostle John Griffith met with me at my home.

We had a wonderful discussion about my answers in the questionnaire and being called into the ministry; the meeting went very well. That evening we stayed at Brother Skip Swanson's home. Brother Tom Jones and his wife, Tava, were with us for the evening as well.

The next morning, as I was getting dressed for Sunday Service, I felt an empty feeling. I felt discouraged, depressed and void of the Spirit of God. I started questioning myself and my calling into the ministry: "Tony, what's this all about? Can you really do this?" It was a horrible feeling. After I got dressed, the Lord put the thought into my mind to read his Word. I picked up my Bible and sat down in the living room. I asked the Lord what I should read. I opened my Bible to 1 Thessalonians, chapter 2, verse 4, where the apostle Paul is speaking as a minister: "But as we were allowed of God to be put in trust with the Gospel, even so we speak; not pleasing men, but God, which trieth our hearts." When I read these words, the Spirit of God came down upon me so strong, that I could not contain the tears. I praised God! The Lord had given me the answer to doubts about my calling.

At that very moment, Brother Tom Jones came into the room. He knew nothing about what had happened that morning. Brother Tom said to me, "Brother Tony, I was thinking this morning about you. If you ever are feeling down and empty and you do not know what to say or do, go to Alma, chapter 31, verse 5, where it says. 'It was expedient that they should try the virtue of the Word of God.' Yes, Brother Tony, inquire of the Word of God."

Again, I could not hold back the tears. This was a confirmation to me that morning that I should not doubt my calling.

Ordaination of Tony Micale

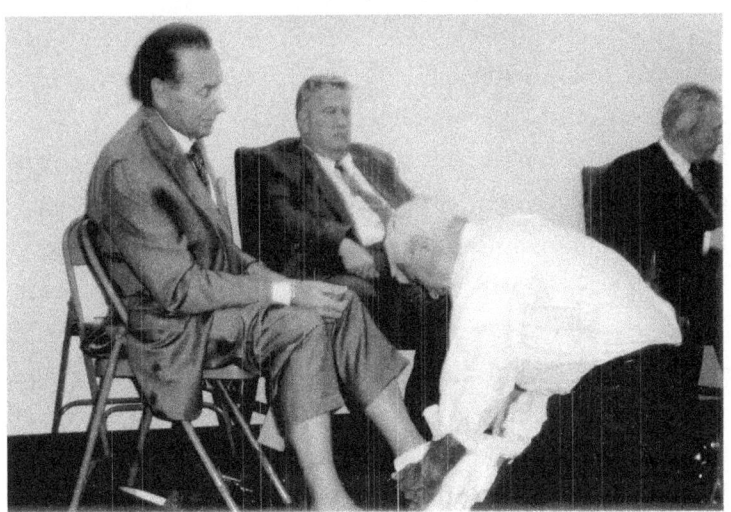

Brother Sam Risola washing my feet at the Ordaination

The enemy of my soul had put doubt in my mind, but the Lord came to my aid and made me to understand that I was truly called by Him. Brother Tom was used that morning by God to confirm and clear up the matter. I am constantly amazed at the goodness of God, who will never fail us.

At my ministerial board review, tongues were spoken by Apostle John Griffith with the interpretation given, "You have been called of God into the ministry"—a man of God. As the song says, "My God, How GREAT Thou Art." Thy Mercy is overflowing!

After being approved by the ministerial board to be ordained a minister in the Church of Jesus Christ, I had to wait for the day of my ordination. The waiting was hard and I was a little nervous! I was very excited on one hand, and on the other hand, I didn't know what to expect. The thought of being called into the ministry had been on my mind for some time, and all kinds of thoughts went through my head. I would say to the Lord, "Let Thy will be done in my life; I am satisfied with whatever you give me to do for you." Without the Lord's Spirit, I knew my ministry would not be fruitful.

The day of my ordination, August 28, 2011, was filled with anxiety and excitement for me and I am sure, for my friends and family who joined us for the service. The Cape Coral Church building was full with about 75 people attending. My daughter, Linda, played the piano and sang, "Your Great Name." It was beautiful and inspiring. Brother Phil Benyola also played the piano beautifully, as he always does. Many family members and friends traveled a great distance to share this day with us. It was wonderful that all my children were present. I thought to myself, "Is this really happening?"

Brother Apostle John Griffith gave a wonderful talk on my calling and duty before man and God. He used Scriptures to show what it means to be a servant and what was expected from me. The words sunk deep into my heart and mind. Brother Sam Risola, an Evangelist in the Church and dear friend, washed my feet. Brother Phil Benyola confirmed me into the ministry. Other visiting Brothers gave wonderful words of

Lydia and I speaking at the Ordaination

encouragement and support. I am also thankful to my son, Anthony, for taking movies and pictures of the service. This was a weekend to remember. The House of God and our home were full of family, friends, and the spirit of the occasion.

The week following my ordination, I had an experience during the Sunday service. That weekend, Cape Coral hosted the Missionary Benevolence Association (MBA) and the Regional Ladies Circle (RLC). That morning Brother Kevin Murphy opened the service from the Book of Mormon. I mistakenly opened the Scriptures to Mormon, chapter 9, verse 21, where it says, "Behold, I say unto you that whosoever believeth in Christ, doubting nothing, whatsoever he shall ask the Father in the name of Christ, it shall be granted him; and this promise is unto all, even unto the ends of the earth." I felt the Spirit of God strongly as I read this verse, then I realized I was in the wrong place and that Brother Kevin was speaking from the Moroni.

At the end of the service, Brother Chuck Maddock called for anyone who needed prayer. We prayed for many that day. One of them was a young man age 32, Joey Ferguson. Joey was mentally handicapped and had colon cancer. At his last visit to the doctor in Michigan, they were told that it was hopeless for him and to put him in hospice. As we were praying for him, the Lord brought me back to the 21st verse in chapter 9 of the Book of Mormon that I had mistakenly read earlier. Again, I felt a strong Spirit from God. I gave my testimony at the time to the Elders and congregation of this experience. About a month later, Joey's mother, Sharon, gave a testimony that new tests taken on Joey showed a 50 percent reduction in the size of the tumor. The doctors were very pleased with his progress. Joey's life was extended for four months, but the cancer spread and he eventually passed away from liver cancer. Looking back on this experience, I believe the Lord was showing me that He would extend Joey's life for a short time. GOD IS THE SAME YESTERDAY, TODAY AND FOREVER.

In the following weeks, I had the privilege of performing the ordinances of the Church. I remember the first time I served communion to the members. It was a wonderful experience and I could not stop the tears as I went from one member to the next. What a joy and honor to serve the bread and the wine and to remember the Lord. This represented the blood Jesus spilled and His body broken on the cross for our sins. We could never repay Him. The Lord asks so little from us and gives so much.

The next time I served communion, I spilled some wine on the table and missed a few members. I was very upset with myself, but after the meeting the Brothers encouraged me and told me that this happens to every Elder. I also had the privilege the next Sunday to pray for a Brother and Sister who needed help from the Lord. This was a wonderful experience.

My first anointing happened when I least expected it. Brother Skip told me to always carry my blessed oil with me because I will never know when it will be needed. I was flying home from Philadelphia, Pennsylvania and Sister Lydia called me to tell me that a dear friend named Bill Detra had been hit by a car while riding his bicycle to work. Bill's back and nine of his ribs were broken and his throat and lungs were pierced. Sister Lydia arranged for a friend to pick me up at the airport and rushed me to the hospital. Bill was in the intensive care unit. We talked for a while and I asked him if he wanted prayer. Bill replied, "Yes, I need prayer." I anointed his head with oil and asked the Lord to heal him and take away his pain. The room was Spirit-filled. As I was praying for him, Bill fell asleep. When we visited him the next day, Bill told us that when he awoke, the hospital staff asked him if he needed anything. Bill told them, "No, I feel such a peace upon me." I am happy to say that the Lord has answered our prayers and he is recovering well. God is able if we only trust him.

It is hard to describe the joy I feel since my ordination. Brother John Griffith has taken over my training for the next two years. I really appreciate the time he and others are taking in helping me to be the best I can be. I attended the General Church Conference in October 2011 for the first time as an ordained Elder. It was a wonderful experience. I have attended Church conferences for many years, but this one will be unforgettable. I am thankful for the Brothers who took the time to come over to me and say how happy they were when they heard that I was called into the ministry. The unity and love of the Brothers and Sisters is what keeps us together.

A few weeks later in October of 2011, Sister Lydia and I

traveled to Italy with Brother John and Sister Caryl Di Battista and Brother Ron Mazzeo on a planned missionary trip. We spent twelve days visiting the Saints in Cala Gonone and San Demetrio, where we have established the Churches that I have written about earlier. It truly was a blessing for me to be able to fulfill the ordinances of the Church in Italy. The Saints there gave me a standing ovation, they were so happy for me. Their love for us is unconditional. It would take to much space to write all the blessings we experienced that trip. This was my fourteenth trip to Italy. The Lord truly poured out his blessings on us as we fellowshipped together.

When we returned from this trip I was talking to Simone, a manager who works for me, about the trip and my ordination. As we were talking, I remembered that she had a child earlier in the year. I asked her if she wanted me to bless her baby, who is named Alani. I explained our beliefs. She replied, "Would you do that for me?!" I said, "Absolutely, it would be an honor for me to bless your baby! It would be my first blessing of a child." We were both excited about it. I spoke with the Brothers at the Mt. Laurel Branch and we decided to make it into a special day. On the day of the blessing, Simone brought twelve visitors to Church and we had 62 people in attendance. After the service, we had a wonderful lunch served and we had time to get to know the visitors. They said that they enjoyed themselves and would come back. That is our hope. We have so much to offer to the world in the Church. We have to step out in faith. God will give the increase if we do.

On March 5, 2012, Sister Lydia and I returned to Italy along with the Italy missionary team, Brother John and Sister Caryl Di Battista, Brother Ron Mazzeo, and Alex Gentile for two weeks. This was my fifteenth trip in six and half years. There was a lot of opposition before going on this trip. The week before I came down with a chest cold and Lydia had an awful bout with stomach pain, on top of her just getting over surgery a month earlier. That weekend before we were leaving, we were both in bed. We thank God that he gave us the strength to travel, this time with a stop in Milan.

Lydia recovered, but I got worse. The next ten days were very difficult for me. This was one of the worst bronchitis-type colds I have ever had. I prayed to the Lord to help me through the trip, so I could be a help to the Brothers in Italy. I thank God that on that first Sunday in Milan, Brother Alex asked me and Brother Ron to open the service. The Lord had answered my prayer and I felt well enough on Sunday to open the service. I spoke on the third chapter of 1st John, "What manner of love the lord has for us that we would be called the sons and daughters of God." Afterwards, we had a wonderful time of prayer, as many attending asked for prayer for their many needs. The Brothers and Sisters in Milan really appreciate our visits. They do not have regular meetings because of too many problems to mention. It is our prayer that we can open a mission in Milan with regular meetings soon.

We had traveled from Rome to Milan by train, then from Milan to Naples by airplane, and by car to the branch in San Demetrio were we spent six days. After our visit to San Demetrio, it was a six-hour drive back to Rome to return to the States. The entire trip was approximately 12,000 miles. These trips are not for the faint of heart; they are very hard and tiring. Nonetheless, we had a wonderful trip visiting the Brothers and Sisters and friends during the week. We encouraged them, prayed for the sick and their needs, which are many.

On our last Sunday there, we had another blessed service. We spoke about the woman who touched the hem of the Lord's garment and was healed of her affliction. The Lord once more gave me and the Brothers liberty in speaking. After the service one of our visitors, Angela, asked me to baptize her when we return to Italy. I asked her mother, "How about you?" and she replied, "Yes, me too!" What a blessing we felt as we saw the Lord doing his handiwork and touching someone's heart. This was another first for my ministry.

So we see that the enemy of our souls tried to stop us from going, because he knew the blessings that would be coming from the Lord. There was too much to write about to capture all the events that took place those two weeks. It is enough to say the Lord gave the increase and we arrived home safely.

His Love and Mercy Overflows

ALTHOUGH I TOOK STRONG ANTIBIOTICS FOR THE bronchitis I suffered from in Italy, I never truly recovered when we returned to the United States. I was still very run-down, but I continued to keep a very busy schedule traveling back and forth to Florida almost weekly for my ministry and taking care of my family and business.

At the end of May 2012, Lydia, Chiara and I made a trip to California to help Chiara get settled in a summer program for college. Once she was settled, we visited our friends, Brother Jim and Sister Lynette Huttenberger, in Irvine, California, then spent the weekend with them at a Church campout high in the Sierras. What a wonderful time we had! Brother Jim and Sister Lynette always make you feel at home, as do the Brothers and Sisters in California. It was beautiful in the mountains and very cold—only 36 degrees when we arrived. I was asked to open the preaching service on Sunday morning. The Lord gave me liberty in speaking and we all felt God's blessings.

When we returned home in June 2012, I became ill with pneumonia. It had been one sickness after another since February. My health really started to suffer and deteriorate. My strength had left me. Without going into a lot of detail, I visited my doctor and found out I also had a urinary tract infection. This started me on my fifth round of strong antibiotics since suffering with the bronchitis/flu in Italy. I had blood work done on a Friday and we traveled back to Florida on Saturday. I was completely exhausted and dehydrated.

The following Monday morning, I received a call from my doctor who told me to go straight to the emergency room at Sarasota Memorial Hospital. The illnesses from the last four months had taken their toll on me. My blood counts were the worst they had ever seen and my kidneys were not functioning properly. I have never felt so bad in my life.

While I was in the hospital, I started reading the Scriptures. I opened to Philippians 1 and as I read in the sixth verse, the Apostle Paul said, "being confident of this very thing, that he which hath begun a good work in you will perform it until the day of Jesus Christ," I felt the spirit of God and the tears could not be held back. I knew then that the Lord was in the matter. I was greatly uplifted. The next thing we did was call the Brothers to put the word out to the entire Church to pray for me. What a joy it is to know that you have the Saints of God praying for you throughout the world!

I spent the next week in the hospital recovering and taking tests to find out what was causing my body to collapse. After many X-rays, CT scans and tests, they said the Crohn's disease in my small intestine was badly inflamed. As a result, I was not getting the nutrients from my food to give me strength and keep my blood levels up. I had become malnourished. The doctors explained that all the medication I had been taking the past four months was a big factor in my current condition. Through a CT scan of my intestine, they found that a section of it was very narrow and another section was greatly inflamed and enlarged bigger than my stomach. The doctors at Sarasota Memorial recommended immediate surgery to correct the problem. We were in shock. I decided not to have the surgery in Florida and to see my surgeon in Philadelphia who had operated on my small intestines four years before. The doctor in Florida said it would take a miracle to not have surgery done.

After five days in the hospital, my blood count and strength had recovered enough to send me home for the weekend and then return to Philadelphia on the following Tuesday. That night as I lay in bed in the hospital I could not sleep. The shock was overwhelming. I clearly remember the last surgery I had and it was terrible. I was praying and could not stop thinking about what was going to happen. The Lord inspired me to think about the Sunday service I would be missing at the Cape Coral, Florida mission. Brother Scott Griffith was sending Elders there to cover for me, but I thought I would really like to see everyone before I left.

Then the thought came to me, why not invite everyone to come to our home on Sunday? We could have a service there and then lunch for all afterward. We had done this several times before with great success. I became excited about this and texted my wife at six o'clock in the morning. I wrote, "Honey, if you really want to make me happy, could we have Church service and lunch in our home on Sunday?" I knew she had spent the day before making a big pot of spaghetti sauce and meatballs. After the hospital food, I was really looking forward to my wife's sauce! Sister Lydia answered back, "Whatever you want, Tony." She knew how much it would mean to me. What a blessing my wife is to me and our family. She has been through a lot herself lately with a health problem. This would be a lot of work for her.

Fortunately for us, my brother-in-law, Phil, who is also a member of our church and a great cook, stepped in and really helped. We made the calls and Brother Scott Griffith approved it. Some thought this would be too much and tiring, but I knew it was God's will. We took this opportunity to invite friends. Five of them attended, along with nineteen members of the Church. This was also a chance to show our friends the Church in action. Twenty-four Brothers, Sisters and friends attended in all. We had a beautiful service.

At first, we did not have a piano player but the Lord was again in the matter. Brother Justin Severson and his wife, Tina, unbeknownst to me, were in the area for a funeral and wanted to see me and visit Cape Coral. He called Brother Skip Swanson, who happened to be out of town at the time. Skip told Brother Justin that I was in the hospital but did not know if I had been released. Brother Justin prayed that morning that the Lord would find a way for him to see me. They started heading for the Cape Coral mission from the Venice, Florida area. After a short time, Sister Tina noticed that they were heading north instead of south to Cape Coral! Brother Justin would not listen to Sister Tina telling him over and over again he was going the wrong way. Finally Sister Tina called Sister Dorene Kugal, who was at our house already, for directions to Cape Coral. She told Sister Tina that the Cape Coral Mission was closed and that we were all at Brother Tony and Sister Lydia's house! Sister Tina responded, "That is wonderful! We are only a few minutes away from Sarasota and we will be right there." The Lord had guided Brother Justin north instead of south to our home. This was an answer to his prayer. The Lord would find me for him so he would be able to pray for me and see me. When they arrived, we also learned that Sister Tina plays the piano! Another answered prayer. What an awesome God we have who fills our every need!

Brother Kevin Murphy and Brother Dee Eutsey, Sr. had also traveled from the Forest Hills branch to support the service and now we had Brother Justin as well. Brother Justin was asked to open the service and he was followed by Brother Kevin. The Spirit of God was with them and our meeting was blessed. The testimonies were full of God's goodness and blessings to them. They remembered the meetings in the Saints' homes in the old days and the blessings they felt. Many asked for prayer as I did. Brother Justin anointed me and asked the Lord to heal me. What power there is in the Gospel of Jesus Christ and his Church! As we read in the Scripture, as the Saints met united often together in the Church, the blessings of God were with them. I also want to thank Brother Joe Manes who spent the weekend with us. He showed me love and comfort when I needed it. This is the love of the Saints of God.

That Sunday night I had my first good night's sleep in a long time. The next day, I started to feel good and much stronger. I said to my wife, "Honey something has happened, I am feeling so much better." We traveled back to Philadelphia on Tuesday with no problem. I had been getting stronger each day as I waited to see the surgeon on Thursday. On Wednesday (July

11), I said to my wife, "I am feeling great and I am not having any problem with my stomach or anything else. Maybe I don't need surgery but just treatment for the Crohn's disease." This statement was prophetic of things to come. We both said, "Let's see what God can do."

On Thursday, we visited the surgeon, Doctor Scott Goldstein, who is the top doctor for this type of surgery in Philadelphia. Dr. Goldstein operated on me four years ago. Without looking at any data or pictures, he started to ask me why I was there and what was the problem. I gave him the history of my illness for the past ten days. I continued to tell him about my hospital stay and the fact that the doctors in Sarasota, Florida, wanted to operate on me for a major problem in my intestinal tract that had to be removed. I explained, "They said I might have to have a bag outside of me for awhile if they could not find good tissue to reconnect to. We were in shock listening to this. I told them I wanted to come and see you for this surgery. They told us only a miracle would prevent it."

Dr. Goldstein then examined me and said, "Let me ask you a few questions. How do you feel?" I told him that I felt fine. He continued, "Are you having any problems in your stomach or intestinal tract?" I said no. He asked, "Does your stomach swell up and your food and bile repeat on you?" I said no. Then Dr. Goldstein said, "Why would I operate on you and for what? I do not need to even look at these CT Scans or X-rays. There is nothing wrong with you."

Lydia and I looked at each other in disbelief. We stood there half-crying and half-smiling and said, "This is unbelievable. The Lord had answered all of our prayers. A miracle of God has just occurred." I kept asking him questions, like, "But

Doctor, what about what they said in Florida that they saw on the X-rays." He responded, "What can I do to convince you? Listen, we will look at the X-rays, but I must tell you from what I see looking at you and your answers to my questions, you do not need surgery. I will call you over the weekend after I have read the X-rays, but unless I see something that shows a blockage, you do not need surgery. Go home and relax."

We left the doctor's office praising God but still in disbelief. The next day, we received a call from Dr. Goldstein and he said, "Tony have a great weekend, you are fine. There is nothing wrong, there is no blockage and your Crohn's disease is not even active." He explained that part of the problem may have been that the doctors in Florida did not understand the type of surgery he had done. Again when I started asking him questions, he cut me off and said, "Tony please relax and go see your stomach doctor. Enjoy the weekend, you are fine. I will send you the X-rays and you can show them to your doctor in New Jersey." There are two sets of X-rays a week apart: one in Florida and one taken in New Jersey this week (week of July 9).

One week ago I was in despair and now after the anointing on Sunday by Brother Justin, Brother Kevin, Brother Dee and the prayers of the Brothers and Sisters, the Lord heard our prayers and healed me of this disease problem. We are home rejoicing and praising God for this miracle in our lives. This is one more testimony of the Lord keeping his promise that he will always be with us. This reminds me of the words of the song, "How Many Times Has He Answered Your Prayers." I think back now again of the Scripture I read from the Apostle Paul when I first entered the hospital, "Being confident of this very thing, that he which hath begun a good work in you will perform it until the day of Jesus Christ."

My recovery has been nothing less than miraculous. A **Miracle** is described in the dictionary as:

An effect or extraordinary event in the physical world that surpasses all known human or natural powers and is ascribed to a supernatural cause.

Such an effect or event manifesting or considered as a work of God.

A Wonder, A Marvel

THIS EXPERIENCE WAS ALL OF THE ABOVE. Whatever days I have left will be in the service of my fellowman and the **Lord Jesus Christ.** I remember my father telling me to always try to keep the commandments of the Lord and He will bless me and prosper me. My father put this in my heart many times and I never have forgotten it. With God all things are possible; my life is proof of this. His love and mercy are overflowing. He took me from where I was to where I am—a minister in **The Church of Jesus Christ** with all the power and blessings from above.

Now in August 2012, it has been almost a year since my ordination. As I mentioned earlier, I am working on a two-year training program under the direction of the Apostles of the Church. I truly have learned a lot and made my share of mistakes. Now I know why they put you through the training program! It is hard to explain the impact my ordination has had on my life. Nothing is the same as before, because the responsibility of the ministry takes first place in your life. At times I am overwhelmed with my calling. I am responsible for the spiritual welfare of the members of the Church and it has been a privilege to serve my fellow man.

It is now the last week of November 2012, my 75th birthday is here. It is hard to believe how fast the years go by. As I end writing this part of my journey with God in my life, it is my hope and prayer that whomever reads this book along with my children and future grandchildren will know a little more about their grandfather, the joys, the many mistakes, the many successes, and from my life they might learn an make the right choices and decisions in life. And most of all to put God first in everything they do. I believe Solomon said it all in Ecclesiastes 12:13-14:

> "Let us hear the conclusion of the whole matter; fear God and keep his commandments; for this is the whole duty of man. For God shall bring every work to judgement, with every secret thing, whether it is good, or whether it be evil. Without the Lord we can do nothing."

It is my hope that someday we will all meet in the Paradise of God and live with the Lord forever.

Dio Vi Benedica

Therefore, having been justified by faith, we have peace with God through our Lord Jesus Christ, through whom also we have access by faith into this grace in which we stand, and rejoice in hope of the glory of God.

—Romans 5:1-2

Acknowledgments

A word from Tony;

I would like to take this opportunity to thank my family and friends for their assiatance in compling this book.

- ༄ The Apostle Paul Benyola, for his continued guidance and support.
- ༄ Evangelist John DiBattista, for his inspiration to write this book.
- ༄ My wife Lydia, for the countless hours.
- ༄ My daughter Linda, who did a incredible job organizing , categorizing, making sure my life was put in order, as she could only do. For her beautiful words and the finishing touches.
- ༄ My step-daughter Chiara, for attempting to take on the making of this book until we all realized it was much bigger than we thought.And for always being there when we needed her.
- ༄ My son Anthony,for organizing , finding and burning the CD's of all the pictures.
- ༄ My daughter Alexis, for all her love and support.
- ༄ Beth Winkle, our dear, dear friend, who is always there for us, through laughter and tears, bad spelling and grammer , and who also knew from the beginning this was going to be WAY bigger than we ever imagined.
- ༄ Thank you all! Together, we did it.